THE THAMES AND I

The Thames and I

A MEMOIR OF
TWO YEARS AT OXFORD

———□———

by

Prince Naruhito
CROWN PRINCE OF JAPAN

With a Foreword by
HIS ROYAL HIGHNESS, THE PRINCE OF WALES
and a Preface to the English edition by
HIS IMPERIAL HIGHNESS, THE CROWN PRINCE

English translation by
SIR HUGH CORTAZZI

RENAISSANCE BOOKS

THE THAMES AND I
A MEMOIR OF TWO YEARS AT OXFORD

Originally published in Japanese by Gakushūin Kyōyōshinsho, Tokyo
entitled *Thames to tomo ni*
© 1993 Prince Naruhito, Crown Prince of Japan

First published in English 2006 by Global Oriental
Reprinted 2014

This edition first published 2019 by
RENAISSANCE BOOKS
P O Box 219
Folkestone
Kent CT20 2WP

Renaissance Books is an imprint of Global Books Ltd

© 2019 The Japan Society

ISBN 978-1-898823-98-8 [Paperback]

British Library Cataloguing in Publication Data
A CIP catalogue entry for this book is available
From the British Library

Set in Garamond 11.5 on 13pt.
Printed and bound by CPI Antony Rowe

CLARENCE HOUSE

It gives me great pleasure to introduce this enjoyable and perceptive Memoir, which The Crown Prince of Japan wrote in 1992 and which has now been translated into English. The book shows a keen eye, a delicate sense of humour, an enviable desire to be involved in a wide variety of activities and a power of description which gives the reader interest and enjoyment.

There is a close friendship between the United Kingdom and Japan, which is reflected in the solid bond between the Imperial and Royal Families. It always gives us pleasure to welcome members of the Emperor's Family to the United Kingdom and it is marvellous that so many of them have chosen to attend British Universities.

Prince Naruhito clearly enjoyed his time at Oxford, and I thank His Imperial Highness for sharing so much with us in this very readable memoir.

PREFACE TO THE ENGLISH EDITION

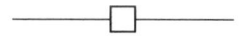

I am very pleased that an English translation of my memoir has now been published. It is twenty years since I left Oxford but I recall fondly the days I spent there as if they took place yesterday. I feel that what I learned whilst I was studying in England during those brief two years has enriched my life a great deal. I shall be pleased if English readers find something of interest in this account of my experiences and impressions.

I am most grateful to Prince Charles, the Prince of Wales, for the interest which he has shown in my book and for the warm message which he has written for the English publication of this memoir. I also wish to express my appreciation for the efforts of all concerned, which enabled this translation to be published. I thank in particular Sir Hugh Cortazzi, the translator, for the zeal and efforts he has put into this project. I would also like to express my appreciation for the help and advice given by others over this publication, especially my mentors Professor Mathias and Dr Highfield.

I hope that this book may contribute even if only in a small way to mutual understanding between Britain and Japan and bring our two countries closer together.

Naruhito

CONTENTS

———□———

Photographs taken by HIH The Crown Prince facing page 76

Foreword by HRH The Prince of Wales	v
Preface to the English edition by HIH Crown Prince Naruhito	vii
Foreword to the Paperback edition by David Warren	xiii
Preface to the Japanese edition (1992)	xv
Translator's Note by Hugh Cortazzi	xvii
The Gakushūin	xviii

1. Ten Days in the Japanese Ambassador's Residence: — 1
Arrival in London — 1
Life in the ambassador's residence — 2
First visit to Oxford — 4
Excursion by the Thames — 5

2. Life in Colonel Hall's House: — 7
I move to Colonel Hall's — 7
Studying English — 8
Life in the Hall household — 12
Second visit to Oxford and call at Professor Mathias's house — 16
Visit to Scotland — 18
Last month at the Halls — 20

3. Entering Oxford: — 24
Arrival at Merton — 24
Before matriculation — 27
University Entrance ceremony — 30

4. About Oxford: 32

'Dreaming spires' 32

'Town and Gown' – A brief history of Oxford University 33

College system 35

Education at Oxford and regular activities in the
University 38

Merton 41

5. Daily Life at Oxford: 46

In the mornings 46

Middle Common Room (MCR) 48

Shopping and the English character 50

Draughts and baths 54

Dinner 54

High table 57

Weekends 60

Family visits 62

With Oxford students 64

6. Cultural Life at Oxford: 73

Films, theatre and music 73

Enjoying chamber music 77

Visits to places associated with musicians:
England and music 82

7. Sport: 85

Rowing 85

Tennis and squash 86

Jogging, climbing, skiing and other sporting activities 92

8. Life as a Research Student at Oxford: 98

Why I decided to do research on the Thames as a highway 98

Professor Mathias 100

Visiting record offices 111

Dr Highfield 115

Preparing my thesis 123

Canals past and future 127

Contents

9. Travels in Britain and Abroad: 129
Weekend drives in the countryside and around Oxford   129
Trips in Britain involving overnight stays   131
Travelling round Europe and meeting European
    Royal Families   135

10. Looking Back on My Two Years' Stay: 137
The English people as I saw them   137
On leaving Britain   141

Postscript   144

Bibliography   146
Index   147

FOREWORD TO THE
PAPERBACK EDITION

by

David Warren
Chairman, The Japan Society, 2012–2018

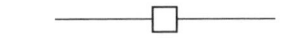

From June 1983 to October 1985, His Imperial Highness Prince Naruhito studied at Merton College, Oxford. In 1993, he published a record of his time there under the Japanese title *Thames to tomo ni*, which was translated into English by the late Sir Hugh Cortazzi as *The Thames and I*. His Highness had become Crown Prince of Japan in 1989 on the death of his grandfather, Emperor Shōwa, and in the spring of 2019 he will himself ascend to the throne as Emperor of Japan, when his father, Emperor Akihito, abdicates. On this occasion, the Japan Society, in collaboration with Renaissance Books, is reissuing His Highness's book, for a new generation of readers.

The Thames and I is a charming and unusual memoir. Both Prince Naruhito's father and grandfather had visited Britain when they had been Crown Prince. But no-one in direct succession to the throne of Japan had ever studied outside Japan before, let alone at a British university. A Prince's life is one of privilege but also, inevitably, one marked by custom and constraint. A student's life is very different. His Highness evokes the life of the University, and particularly his college, with engaging detail and a sensitive memory for his impressions at the time. He describes a student world that many will recognise, wherever they may have studied: getting to know other students, finding one's way around a complex and confusing university town, becoming part of a college community, and settling down to a specific area of research (in Prince Naruhito's case, the River

Thames as a highway and centre of transportation in the eighteenth century) and working in the archives. And, of course, a student's life, even that of Prince Naruhito, who was exceptionally diligent, is not all work: His Highness describes moments of relaxation – the college parties, rowing on the river, the trips to the pub, the outings to cinemas, theatres and concerts, as well as excursions further afield to discover other parts of Britain and Europe.

Running through the book is a fondness for Britain and its traditions and eccentricities, which many British visitors to Japan encounter among the Japanese. His Highness describes Oxford life with a gentle, observant eye, even recording humorously the occasional harmless misadventure. The Oxford in which the Prince lived, before the internet, before digitised libraries, before the advent of mobile telephones, not to mention the ending of single-sex colleges, now seems a long time ago. Much has changed. But His Highness's determination to make the most of his two years in Oxford and his realisation that his experiences there were, as he says, 'irreplaceable', come through very strongly and poignantly. And the sense of friendship between Britain and Japan, and between the British and the Japanese people, emerges as well, in this record of a unique journey across two cultures.

□

The Japan Society wishes to record the generosity of the late Sir Hugh Cortazzi, who shortly before his death in August 2018 expressed a desire that the reprint should be made available as widely as possible and to this end arranged to fund the printing costs of this edition.

PREFACE TO THE
JAPANESE EDITION

———□———

I was at Oxford from the end of June 1983 to early October 1985 and my stay in Britain thus came to roughly two years and four months. 1 had so many experiences during this time that I cannot recount them all here. It is seven years now since I left Oxford and the precious memories of my younger days there come flooding back across the years. I need hardly say how valuable they have been to my way of life today.

However, as my supervisor at Oxford during my studies there, Professor Peter Mathias, wrote in the preface to the Japanese translation of his book *The First Industrial Nation* 'In preparing this preface to a new edition of my book I am writing for Japanese readers about what must seem to them the other side of the world', I too, in recording memories of my two years at Oxford, am writing in Tokyo which is on the other side of the world to Oxford. In writing this preface the thoughts, which race through my mind, are all about my enjoyable life as a student at Oxford. It was, of course, impossible in the brief two years that I lived in Oxford to grasp the whole picture of the university with its diversity and long history. However in the short period that I was at Oxford I had an unforgettable experience. I have tried, as best I can, within the limit of what a single individual can absorb, to describe what I saw, did and thought and I hope that it will contribute to better understanding.

I want to dedicate this account of my two years in Oxford to my parents who made this stay possible. Without their help and support I would not have been able to enjoy to the full the life of a student abroad.

Winter, 1992

TRANSLATOR'S NOTE

———□———

Thames to tomo ni was originally published in Japanese by Gakushūin Kyōyōshinsho in Tokyo in 1993.

Her Imperial Highness, The Crown Princess Masako, had long planned to produce a translation of this book, but owing to her many commitments was unable to do so before the present translation was submitted to His Imperial Highness Crown Prince Naruhito.

When the Prince was at Oxford he was the elder son of the then Crown Prince Akihito who became the Heisei era Emperor in 1989 on the death of the Shōwa era Emperor (Hirohito).

This translation has been made from the Japanese by Sir Hugh Cortazzi. He wishes to record his thanks for all advice received from the Crown Prince's Household and for the valuable suggestions made by Lady Bouchier (Dorothy Britton) and Ms Akiko Machimura on the best way to translate this text. He is also grateful to Professor Mathias, Dr Roger Highfield, Colonel Tom Hall and Dr Carmen Blacker for reading the text and suggesting amendments. Any remaining errors are his responsibility.

A very small number of minor modifications have been made in translating the text to reflect the facts as known to the translator who has added a few explanatory footnotes.

Permission for this translation to be made was given by the Japanese Imperial Household in late 2004.

THE GAKUSHŪIN

The Prince makes various references in the text to the Gakushūin where he had studied in Japan. The Gakushūin University traces its origin to the 'Old Gakushūin' which was established in 1847 in Kyoto as the educational institution of the Imperial Court. The name Gakushūin is made up of three Chinese characters meaning 'to be taught', 'to learn' and 'institution'. In 1877, after the Meiji Restoration, it was re-established in Tokyo as a school for the nobility and was popularly referred to as the Peers School. In 1884 entry to the school was opened to children from outside the ranks of the nobility In 1947 the Gakushūin became an entirely private school to which anyone could gain entry if they passed the entrance examinations. In 1949 the Gakushūin University was established. The university now has some 9,000 students and fourteen departments divided into four separate faculties. It also has a graduate school comprising six separate schools and fourteen specialist courses.

CHAPTER 1

TEN DAYS IN THE JAPANESE AMBASSADOR'S RESIDENCE

□

Arrival in London

I arrived at London's Heathrow airport before dawn on 21 June 1983. I do not remember much about what I could see of London from the aircraft, perhaps because I was sleepy and nervous. The sky in the foreign country in which I was to live for two years looked dull and cloudy and although it was supposed to be summer it felt unexpectedly chilly. I was greeted by Ambassador Hirahara, Mr Elliott, the head of the Far Eastern Department at the British Foreign Office, and one of my cousins Mr Mibu Motohiro who was working in Japan Airline's London Office, and others. After a few minutes in an airport room I was taken by car to the ambassador's residence where I was to stay for ten days.

This was not my first visit to London. I had spent a short time there on my return from visits to Belgium and Spain in 1976. Because I was changing planes I had little time to see London and my memory of that visit was limited to seeing Windsor Castle and the river Thames flowing past, and eating roast beef at a nearby restaurant. I was impressed by Windsor Castle but I was not much impressed by the Thames or the taste of the roast beef. I had a clear memory of looking at the Thames while crossing over it on an old bridge and seeing rubbish floating in dirty water. The taste of the roast beef seemed plain and nothing special.

Now seven years later, as I abandoned myself to the comfortable motion of a motor car, I felt that the curtain was quietly lifting and that I was about to begin an unprecedented two-year stay in a foreign country and the drama of an unknown yet exciting experience as a foreign student. Looking out of the car windows I thought that London had a solemn atmosphere and that the buildings looked impressive and serene. The environment of the Ambassador's residence was tranquil and impressed me very favourably. After taking a rest in the morning I went out again in the afternoon for a drive around the city. This gave me a second chance to see the Thames. Looking at the river up close, with buildings such as the Houses of Parliament, Big Ben and St Paul's Cathedral providing a backdrop, I realized for the first time what an important part the river plays in the London scene. The River Thames – from my former image of it as a rather dirty river, to its existence as a necessary, vital element in the London scene – rapidly began to captivate my mind. And at that point I had no idea that the Thames would become the theme of my studies and research while I was in Britain.

Life in the ambassador's residence

My stay in the residence, thanks to the arrangements made by Ambassador and Mrs Hirahara, was a very pleasant one. This was a good opportunity for me to learn more about Britain.

On 22 June, the day after my arrival, I was able to watch the opening of parliament. The solemn ceremony took place in the House of Lords in the presence of Her Majesty Queen Elizabeth and her consort Prince Philip, Duke of Edinburgh. The ceremony began with the formal entry of the Queen and Prince Philip into the chamber where the peers dressed in their resplendent robes were waiting. In due course the Queen's messenger proceeded to the House of Commons and speaking in a loud voice knocked on the door of the chamber. After he had twice been refused entrance, on the third occasion the door was opened and the members of the lower house proceeded as a body to the upper house. I realized that the historical rationale behind the opening of the door of the House of Commons at the third summons and the whole proceedings lay in the puritan revolution, when the House of Commons achieved its independence from the crown and became the central organ of government. Soon, the members of the lower house dressed in their ordinary clothes made their appearance. I noted among them Mrs Thatcher, the Prime Minister. The Queen read out the speech setting out the policies of the second Thatcher administration. The ceremony ended after about thirty minutes. This was the first occasion for me to appreciate that Britain was indeed a land of tradition.

That evening I called at her invitation on Princess Alexandra at St James's Palace. This was the first time I had met the Princess but she made me feel very much at home by the informal and friendly way in which she received me. The following day I was to call at Buckingham Palace where I had been invited to tea by Her Majesty the Queen. Prince Andrew and Prince Edward were present and I had a pleasant time in a relaxed atmosphere. The Queen asked what I was going to do in Britain and spoke among other things about her visit to Japan. Prince Andrew spoke about his service in the navy and Prince Edward about his life as a student. Of course I felt rather nervous but the conversation was very informal and enjoyable. I wondered how 'Tea' was served in England, but the Queen kindly poured the tea herself. I also noted that sandwiches and cakes were served with Tea. On the 24th I was invited to lunch by Princess Anne at her house in Gloucestershire. I made a courtesy call on Princess Margaret and signed the book at the Queen Mother's. I was very fortunate to be able to meet so many members of the Royal Family so soon after my arrival. I was also able at this time to meet the relevant British Foreign Office officials, the Earl and Countess of Mansfield from Scotland who were my personal guarantors, Colonel Tom Hall, with whom I would be staying for three months to study English before entering the university, Sir Rex Richards, the warden of Merton College at Oxford where I would be studying, and Professor Peter Mathias from All Souls, who would be my academic supervisor. My meeting with these latter two gentlemen before I had even entered the university increased my expectations of life at Oxford. Sir Rex Richards struck me as a courteous English gentleman and Professor Mathias seemed a typical scholar. I also benefited from briefings about Britain which members of the Embassy in turn gave me over breakfast.

First visit to Oxford

I first went to Oxford on 24 June. I still have a clear recollection of that visit. I went by car along the M40 to Oxford which lies some 90 kilometres to the North West of London. In the countryside, which looked as if it was covered by a green carpet, I occasionally saw sheep grazing. I spent a peaceful hour contemplating this poetic and bucolic scene. Soon after turning off the main road, we were driving along a narrow country road and passing through villages with rows of stone buildings. Suddenly, I caught sight of the tower of Magdalen of which I had seen a photograph. Soon we reached Merton. There Sir Rex Richards, whom I had met on the previous day, was waiting for me and he showed me round the various college buildings. While looking at this diverse group of old buildings where I would be studying in the future I was moved in an inexplicable way. During our tour Sir Rex introduced me to a scholarly person with white hair and thick spectacles. He seemed to be deeply absorbed in the study of some book, but as soon as Sir Rex spoke to him he jumped up and shook hands. He was Dr Roger Highfield, the scholar, who would be my tutor at Merton. My first impression of him was that he was rather frightening. Sir Rex no doubt introduced us at this time as he wanted us to get to know one another. Dr Highfield soon returned to his desk and his books. For some reason he left a deep impression on me.

The warden also showed me the 'real tennis' court nearby (for an explanation of 'real tennis' please see the chapter on sports). I was also shown the room which I would be using during my two years at the college, but it was under repair and I could see that there were holes everywhere. Although the college was on holiday I saw various students wandering around. As we passed the warden spoke to each of them. He seemed to know them all by name and through this I began to recognize the merits of the college system. This was probably due in part to the warden's character but also reflected the size of the college which allowed him to remember each student. Although my visit to Merton was a short one I felt greatly attracted by the atmosphere of Oxford and the college. As I was driven back in the car and looked out at Christ Church and the various other colleges on the High Street, I felt very fortunate that I would be able to spend two years here.

I should explain how it came about that out of Oxford's many colleges I entered Merton. It had been left to the British government to decide both the university and college where I was to study. I heard that after some deliberation Merton had been chosen. The reasons were that Sir Rex Richards, the respected vice-chancellor of the University, was the warden of Merton, which was among the oldest colleges in Oxford, it was small enough to enable me to make friends easily and had a good academic reputation. Everyone takes a favourable view of his own college, but looking back nine years later I am convinced that Merton was indeed the right choice. I also heard that the presence at Oxford of Professor Mathias had been an important factor in choosing Oxford rather than Cambridge.

Excursion by the Thames

On 25 June, the day after my visit to Oxford, I made a trip to see various sights on the Thames some half-way between London and Oxford. I lunched that day with Ambassador Hirahara and other Embassy officials at a hotel at Goring-on-Thames. It was the right weather for a walk; so we went out into the hotel garden after lunch and followed a footpath by the river. There were many boats on the Thames that day. The white boats sailing on the river seemed to go so well with the brick-coloured bridge not far off while the blue of the river in the sunshine created a truly attractive scene. And I loved the sight of the various groups sitting on the river bank chatting and laughing.

We went on to Henley-on-Thames. There I learnt that Henley was famous as the place where the Royal Regatta was held, but I was particularly impressed by the beauty of the colours of the façades of the houses by the river. At one place on the river, where there is a wooden bridge, I gazed out over the river and realized how different the Thames is to Japanese rivers. The Thames does not have a dry flood plain[1] and flows calmly between the banks which are part of

---

[1] As many Japanese rivers do

the land beside the river unlike Japanese rivers with their concrete embankments.

The next place we visited was Marlow. From *'The Compleat Angler' Hotel* where we stopped for tea I enjoyed another fantastic view of the Thames with its suspension bridges, the churches across the river and the many flowers which added to the charm of the scenery. Thus, as I came into contact with the river I began to feel a strong affection for the Thames and the image of a dirty river which I had had in the past was completely dissipated.

In addition, while I was staying at the ambassador's residence I was taken on excursions in the South of England, to Brighton, the white cliffs of Beachy Head, Hastings, famous for the battle of the Norman Conquest of 1066, as well as to Canterbury.

CHAPTER 2

LIFE IN COLONEL HALL'S HOUSE

————□————

I move to Colonel Hall's

My twelve days at the ambassador's residence passed quickly. On 3 July I moved to Colonel Hall's house at Chiselhampton outside Oxford. The scenery on the way was familiar as I had travelled this route before on my visit to Oxford, but as I was rather nervous and facing a long 'home-stay' I did not have much inclination to enjoy the scenery. Fortunately, this was not my first experience of a 'home-stay'. In my third year at middle school I had made my first visit overseas to Australia where a 'home-stay' had been part of the trip, but I could not disguise my apprehension in facing a long three-month 'home-stay'.

Colonel Hall's house was a splendid three-storey brick building and it seemed somewhat oppressive. The porch was not far from the gate, but I soon recognized that a spacious garden lay behind the house. I was greeted at the porch by Tom Hall, his wife, Mariette, and their three children, Lucy, Edward and John. I was struck by the size and height of the entrance hall which went up to the second floor. There were various books on the hall table; on one side there was a piano and around the hall were Hall's work-room, the sitting-room, and the dining-room. After we had exchanged greetings Mrs Hall showed me to my room on the first floor. The room had its own bathroom and WC. On the walls there were decorated plates and pictures of birds. From the window I could see the large farm managed by Hall where a number of cows were grazing peacefully and green fields stretching as far as the eye could see. When I came out of my room I looked

7

straight down onto the front hall. Soon, lunch was served. In addition to members of the Hall family, Ambassador Nakagawa who had been appointed to accompany me to Britain, Ambassador Hirahara, Counsellor Fuji who had been given the task of looking after my affairs during the whole of my stay as a student in Britain, and officials from the Japanese Embassy were present. As it was a warm day the table had been laid outside on the terrace. This, my first experience of British home cooking, exceeded all my expectations.

After lunch, I received representatives of the Japanese press in the garden. According to the record which I have the correspondents took pictures of me looking at the horses brought by acquaintances of Colonel Hall and of my taking a walk. After the meeting with the press was over Ambassadors Nakagawa and Hirahara and the others departed and I was left alone in the Hall household. In the evening Colonel Hall invited me to swim in the heated pool in the garden and John showed me how to play croquet, which is similar to the Japanese game of 'gate ball'. At this time of year it is light in Britain until quite late and it was still light when the evening meal was served at 7.30. During the meal Colonel Hall suggested that I look outside. There I saw a fox. Sadly, I do not recall anything about the conversation at dinner that evening except the fox. However, Colonel Hall, his wife and children seemed good people who treated me kindly and I thought I would be able to get by during the three months ahead of me. The first day in the Hall household had seemed rather long, but when I went upstairs to go to bed the Colonel took me to my room and said: 'Good night Hiro,[1] Welcome to our home.' I then realized that the day had ended without mishap and I felt a surge of relief.

Studying English

One of the main purposes of my stay with Colonel Hall before entering university was to improve my English. Colonel Hall, who had been an honorary ADC to the Queen,[2] ran a language school

---

[1] Hiro was the personal name which the Prince used while at Oxford.
[2] Colonel Hall has told me that he was not an ADC to the Queen, but was for eighteen years a Gentleman at Arms in the Queen's bodyguard. Hugh Cortazzi.

and had established a school in Japan. The reason why the British government had recommended that I study with him before I went to Oxford was probably because he managed a language school and this meant that I could study at his home. My language teachers were Mr and Mrs Corcos who taught at Colonel Hall's school and had had experience of teaching in Japan. I met them on the day after my arrival and I had a very favourable impression of them.

The arrangements were for me to receive two hours tuition in the mornings and in the afternoons with each of them in turn. The lessons were held in the basement. At first, to learn practical expressions used in daily life in England an English conversation book was used. To improve my understanding of spoken English I listened to the BBC morning news and to help my reading ability emphasis was placed on understanding newspaper articles. At the beginning, I could hardly understand at all the BBC news on the radio, but I had less difficulty with television news and depending on the subject matter was able to grasp the meaning straight away. After listening to the news on the radio and watching it on TV I had to answer questions, sometimes orally and sometimes in writing, about what I had heard and seen. The same arrangements applied to newspaper articles. As homework I had to keep a diary in English about what I had been doing that day. The first task on the following day was to read through and correct what I had written; the appropriate expressions were explained to me and grammatical errors pointed out. This was very helpful to me in learning how to express my thoughts in English. This was not all that my lessons consisted of. All sorts of materials were used from time to time. On the ground floor tea was served in between lessons. This was poured by the teachers but I noticed that Diana [Corcos] was better at this than her husband Philip [Corcos]. It only consisted of putting a tea bag in the teapot and pouring on boiling water, but Philip almost always managed to scald himself or do something else untoward.

In addition to lessons inside there were occasional lessons outside. One day, we visited the prehistoric monuments at Stonehenge and Salisbury cathedral. While looking round these sites I studied the pamphlets describing their history and found them very helpful in learning the relevant vocabulary. On the following day, I was questioned in English about the visits; this was useful practice in describing what I had seen. Stonehenge is a collection of huge, ancient stones which look as if they had suddenly appeared in the middle of the grassy plain. One could not help but wonder why and who had built it. Salisbury cathedral, not far away, towers over Salisbury plain; it has the highest and most beautiful spire in Britain which was completed in the middle of the fourteenth century and I was overwhelmed by its impressive appearance. The cathedral is an example of English Gothic. In recent years, there has been speculation about 'mystery circles'[3] in this area.

One of my tasks during my outside lessons was to explore Oxford with the help of a booklet explaining the history of the city. In St Mary's Church I tried my hand at brass-rubbing. It entailed placing a sheet of paper on the ancient relief portraits carved into the brass plaques on the graves of those buried there and rubbing black wax onto the paper so that the image appeared on the sheet. Although the plaques were not the real thing but small size copies for tourists I found the process of brass-rubbing a fascinating one.

Among the many other places which I visited were the Museum in Oxford, the Royal Observatory at Greenwich and the Canal Museum at Northampton. I learnt a good deal of basic information about canals from seeing actual things in the museum.

Colonel Hall took me to buy stamps in a shop nearby and I learnt how they were sold. I was also taught how to order beer in a pub. To digress, I should like to describe my first experience in a pub. That day Colonel Hall drove me and his elder son Edward to three pubs in the neighbourhood. Colonel Hall guessed that, after I had gone up to Oxford, I would occasionally visit a pub, and thought that it would be useful for me to learn how to order beer and sample the atmosphere of an English pub. I was taught that in an English pub you did not just ask for a glass of beer but asked either for bitter or lager. Bitter is a traditional English beer with a bitter taste and brown in colour. Lager beer is the type normally drunk in Japan. I learnt that one normally ordered beer by the pint (equivalent to 0.57 litres).

---

[3] The Prince was probably referring to the crop circles which appear each year.

A pint is rather less than there is in a bottle of Japanese beer. So in ordering beer one said: 'A pint of bitter, please!' or 'Half a pint of lager, please!'. Still, I had to summon up some courage to give an order. All went well at the first pub we visited. At the second pub the landlord gave me a look implying 'who is this fellow?' The third pub, which lay beside the Thames and had a thatched roof and white walls, was very pretty. It had a pleasant atmosphere and I visited it after I had joined the university. At first, I did not much care for the taste of bitter, but on my first visit ever to a pub I liked the atmosphere very much.

The river Thames provided material for my study of the English language. Of course at that time I had not yet decided to make the study of transport on the Thames the subject of my university thesis. I only decided on this after I had joined the university. But various items of information about the Thames which I gleaned while staying with Colonel Hall were useful to me in my future studies. One of these was a book by John Gagg[4] about canals, which I read with Mrs Corcos. As one of the objectives of my lessons was to improve my ability to read English I would read a section of the book in advance of the lesson and would then answer questions from Mrs Corcos about what I had read. For someone like myself who knew absolutely nothing about canals in Britain this was a very good introduction to understanding the subject.

In addition to knowledge gained from reading, I had the new experience, while I was staying with Colonel Hall, of actually going on the river. One way of going on the river was punting. Punting is used at both Oxford and Cambridge and consists in moving a boat called a punt, which has a flat bottom and a square prow, by using a long pole; the boat can carry about four people and the pole is made of metal. According to my diary the first time I went punting was on 28 July when I had an enjoyable time with Mr and Mrs Corcos punting on the Cherwell which is a branch of the Thames. We boarded the punt at the Cherwell boathouse restaurant. This was the

---

[4] John C.Gagg is the author of two books about canals published in the1970s. One published in London in 1973 was entitled *5000 Miles, 3000 Locks*, the other published in Princes Risborough in 1971 was entitled *250 Waterway Landmarks*.

easy part; I soon found that it was difficult to prevent the boat turning round and round in a circle and I had difficulty in getting it to move forwards. Moreover, the metal pole was heavy to lift and got stuck in the mud at the bottom of the river. So I was in trouble. I noted that some of the boats going in the opposite direction had expert punters while others had novices like me. When going under a bridge one punter had inadvertently lifted his pole so that it struck the arch of the bridge and the pole fell into the river. I was surprised to see a group jump into the river to pull it out.

I did a return trip one day, although not by punt, from Abingdon, some nine kilometres South of Oxford, to Clifton Hampden, a distance of about eight kilometres. En route at a place called Culham we came to a lock and I was interested to see how it operated. A lock is a mechanism to raise or lower a boat on a steeply flowing river or on a canal; this was a small version of the locks on the Panama Canal. The lock gates being opened and shut mechanically we asked the lock-keeper to open the lock for us and with the boat tied to the bank we were able to observe the rise and fall of the water in the lock and how boats passed through. Although there were four other boats waiting at Clifton lock the transit was effected without a hitch. At Clifton Hampden we had lunch in the open air at the *Barley Mow Inn* and got back to Abingdon at about 5 o'clock. The fact that I can recount all this ten years later is because I wrote about my experiences at the time as part of my homework for Mrs Corcos.

Life in the Hall household

Apart from the two-hour sessions of English-language tuition in the mornings and afternoons there was no fixed routine on weekdays and my activities varied from day to day. I got up in the morning before 8 o'clock and had breakfast with the Hall family. I was impressed to see that in addition to toast there were a variety of cereals from which to choose. In addition to cornflakes there were all sorts of other products made from various types of grains. Colonel Hall and Mrs Hall would generally read the newspaper at breakfast and would sometimes summarize the contents for me in an easily understandable way. After breakfast they would go about their daily business and I would return to my room to prepare for my lessons; I would soon go down to the basement. Although it was a basement it was fairly light, quiet and suitable for studying. After my lesson it was time for lunch. The menu differed from day to day. When roast lamb was served Colonel Hall would himself do the carving and dish it out on the plates. In English homes it is customary for the host to carve and serve the meat. With lamb, mint sauce and red currant jelly are served. I recall that on most days lunch was soon over but we had pleasant conversations over the meal. After lunch I returned to my lessons. When these were over my free time began. In the summer weather I enjoyed swimming and tennis and generally relaxed in the sitting-room. Mrs Hall enjoyed classical music. One of her favourite pieces was a Schubert quintet which I liked very much and on many occasions we had lively conversations about it.

In the evenings the Halls would often invite people they knew and I would join them at table. On the evening after my arrival a Dutch couple and their son came round: I had a great deal of difficulty on this occasion in following the conversation. They seemed a very pleasant family but sadly we could not communicate adequately. Later, when I visited Holland, I met them again as they were acquaintances of Queen Beatrice. Fortunately, their son was also studying at Oxford and we were occasionally able to meet. Colonel Hall having been in attendance on the Queen, among their acquaintances was someone who had done work connected with the Queen's horses[5] and whose wife had been lady-in-waiting to the Queen Mother. Also living in the neighbourhood was the younger sister of the Queen of Sweden and her husband. German, American and Canadian friends also called.

During dinner at the Halls' house I would be asked how my English lessons were going and from time to time they would question me about Japan and the Japanese language. Colonel Hall had been to Japan on many occasions in connection with his language school there and all the family were very interested in Japan. I was, for instance,

---

[5] Colonel Hall has explained that the Queen's stud manager was Sir Michael Oswald.

asked about the relationship between the Chinese and Japanese languages and the use of the same characters in both languages, as well as about the Japanese pronunciation of Chinese characters, and the difference between Chinese characters and *hiragana*. I would then write Chinese characters on scraps of paper and explain how they were constructed. It is not easy to explain phrases which are commonplace in Japanese and at first I had some difficulty, but drawing on written materials I gradually learnt to cope. For instance, I showed how a tree was written and explained how to understand how characters were put together, with two trees together meaning a wood and three trees a forest. Colonel Hall had his own seal with two characters reading '*tomi*' and '*horu*'[6] to represent his name Tom Hall. After drinking strong coffee which kept us awake, eating chocolate mints and having an after-dinner drink we used to go on talking late into the evening.

Some evenings we visited the houses of some of the Halls' acquaintances. On the day after I arrived in the Hall household we visited the house of a Mr Barclay, a neighbour, swam, played tennis and had tea. On 14 July there was a barbeque supper at the same house. This was the first time I had been to a dinner outside the Halls' except to the house being used by Counsellor Fuji. The Halls, the Barclays, their son and daughter and the latter's friends were present. The barbecued meat fresh from the grill tasted really delicious and the evening was most relaxed and enjoyable. I was soon asked about Japan and in particular its mechanical industries. I did my best to reply in my broken English but it was hard work. Nevertheless, I found the conversation with the other guests of about my age interesting. The Barclays said to me: 'English is not easy at first' and were most kind. I felt that I had had a glimpse of English hospitality.

As I enjoy tennis Colonel Hall occasionally arranged what he called tennis parties. Fortunately, he had a wide circle of acquaintance in the area and I got to know many people through tennis. While staying with the Halls I had other opportunities which I had

---

[6] In Japanese *tomi* means wealth and *horu* dig.

not anticipated to meet new people. For instance, at one of the tennis parties at a neighbour's house I got to know a former Davis Cup player. On his invitation I had the good fortune of being able to play on one of the courts at Wimbledon. At Oxford in 1991 I ran into one of those whom I had met at the first of these tennis parties.

While I was staying with the Halls, apart from studying the English language, I got to know a good deal about England and English life. They did all they could to help me in this. The following are some of the things I remember learning from Hall or his children and which naturally helped me greatly to understand Britain.

On 9 July the Halls' youngest son John was due to graduate from Cheltenham College, an English public school in Gloucestershire and the Halls took me with them to the 'speech day' at the school when the families of the boys who were leaving that term could wander freely around the grounds. I was guided around the grounds by John and his friends. It may well be interesting and enjoyable to live a communal life at a boarding school, but I felt that because school discipline was strict life there must have been quite hard and difficult at times. I also saw the rooms which the boys used. The muddy shirts and socks and old worn desks which I saw seemed typical symbols of dormitory life. However, I was interested for the first time in my life to see what a public school was like. We enjoyed a picnic lunch, which the Halls had brought with them, at a table set up in one corner of the spacious garden. Other tables appeared to be occupied by the families of other leavers while nearby young girls wearing smart straw hats were wandering by. It was indeed a peaceful scene.

A particularly vivid memory is the village fête which was held not far from where the Halls lived. That day Colonel Hall arranged for me to be accompanied by his elder son Edward. As the word 'fête' suggests it was a happy occasion: there were various games, and food and drink were on sale. But I made a frightful blunder at the fête in a game involving throwing Wellington boots. The game in England is called 'Wellington' whereas the similar game in France is called 'Napoleon'. Perhaps because I threw the boot with too much energy it flew sideways across a wall. The bystanders who probably regarded me as some strange oriental burst out laughing. I heard later that the boot had grazed a farmer working in a field. Edward, who usually called me Prince Hiro at home, conscious of the circumstances and not wanting to embarrass me, on this occasion tactfully just called me Hiro.

Very recently, I met someone in Tokyo who said he had met me at Oxford. He was the owner of the place where the fête had been held. I had totally forgotten this, but he had not known who I was that day and had asked me 'Where are you from?' I had replied 'From Tokyo'. He then asked me 'From where in Tokyo?' and when I had replied 'From the centre of the city' he had guessed who I was. Even so it had been a good day. It would be impossible in Japan to go to a place where hardly anyone would know who I was. It is really important and precious to have the opportunity to be able to go privately at one's own pace where one wants.

Second visit to Oxford and call at Professor Mathias's house

On 26 July, I was invited by Professor Mathias to lunch at All Soul's where he was a fellow. This was the first time that I had ever had a meal in college and sitting next to Professor Mathias I felt rather nervous. The dining hall at All Soul's is not very large. The other members of the college seemed to be happily enjoying their meal. Among them I noticed one or two who looked like Japanese and who might have been university teachers. I was able to choose from the menu and ordered first a bean soup followed by a meat dish which looked tasty and was recommended by Professor Mathias. It turned out to be liver and had a strong smell. I should have taken notice when Professor Mathias had told me that it was liver. While I was eating two scholars who sat opposite to us and whose names I remember well were Professor Needham and Dr Simmonds. Professor Needham who spoke a good deal and was wearing a Merton tie seemed to be very attached to the college. Dr Simmonds, on the other hand, was rather taciturn and I was lost for words after greeting him with the words 'how do you do?' At this stage it could not be expected that I should be able to converse fluently. When I had been introduced to Dr Simmonds by Professor Mathias, he had explained that my grandfather was the Emperor of Japan. This seemed to strike a bell with him and when we had coffee after the meal Dr Simmonds sure enough produced a photograph out of his pocket. This was of my grandfather on the occasion of his visit to Oxford.

A date was fixed for me to visit Professor Mathias's home in Gloucestershire. This was an attractive simple stone-built house. After a delicious lunch with his wife and daughter, the Professor took me on a guided tour of Chedworth Roman Villa where the bath and house built in Roman times had been preserved. I knew that the Romans were accustomed to taking baths but I was surprised to discover that hot-water and cold-water baths were separated. The method of heating the water was ingenious. Professor Mathias politely and kindly explained each feature of the villa and I had a most enjoyable day.

While I was staying with the Halls I took part in various public functions. I shall not forget the day when I was invited to a garden party at Buckingham Palace. This was held on 19 July which was a hot, sunny day. Men wore either black or grey morning coats and grey top hats. Perhaps because it was summer there were a few more grey than black morning coats and the vast majority had grey top hats. The ladies' clothes were gorgeous. There were a number of people among the diplomatic corps and royal household whose faces I recognized. When the Queen, the Duke of Edinburgh, Prince Charles, Princess Diana and other members of the Royal Family came onto the terrace the national anthem was played.

When the national anthem was over paths were opened up through the crowd and the Queen and members of the Royal Family made their way slowly towards the Royal Tent speaking to various people on the way. In the Royal Tent raspberries and other fruits were served with tea and cake. After the Royal Family reached the tent I was asked by members of the household to wait my turn to be called to meet the Queen. Eventually, I was able to exchange greetings with the Queen and the Duke of Edinburgh. After I had told her that I was enjoying my stay in Britain, the Queen said that she had recently attended the opening ceremony of the NEC factory near Edinburgh. She had been much impressed by having to wear an overall which looked like a space suit. The Duke of Edinburgh asked me in a humorous tone why I had chosen to go to Oxford rather than Cambridge. This was probably because he was Chancellor of Cambridge University.

Visit to Scotland

Towards the end of August, about half-way through my stay with the Halls, I went on a visit of a few days to Scotland. On 28 August I went from London to Edinburgh and stayed very comfortably with the Earl of Haddington and his family at Tyninghame castle. At lunch in the dining-room, which was decorated with the portraits of Haddington's ancestors, the visit to the castle twenty-one years ago by Princess Chichibu was mentioned. That evening we went to hear a concert which was part of the Edinburgh Festival. This consisted of a performance by Pinchas Zuckerman of a Brahms Violin sonata and a Brahms Viola sonata. He had chosen to play these pieces as this was the 150th anniversary of the birth of Brahms. This fine concert performance provided an excellent opportunity to appreciate the different tones of the two instruments, violin and viola. On returning to the Haddington's I danced a Scottish reel with members of the family. There were only a few who knew the correct way of dancing the reel. But with the men and women forming a circle and dancing holding hands it was great fun. Lord Haddington who was approaching his eightieth birthday also seemed to enjoy the dancing.

On the following day, I went with the family to visit a ruined castle nearby. From the ruins on the edge of a cliff we had a wonderful view over the sea. In the afternoon, we went into Edinburgh and visited Edinburgh castle and the palace of Holyrood. Looking at these beautiful, attractive and magnificent buildings and fine city I was overcome by solemn feelings as I thought of the dark and sad episodes of Scottish history, memories of which seem to persist silently and even show signs of going on forever. At the same time I felt for a moment the underlying discord even today between England and Scotland. We went on to look down over Edinburgh from a nearby hill. Through the haze we could see the various spires and shapes of the buildings which made up the city of Edinburgh and I realized why Edinburgh is called the pearl of the British Isles. That evening, accompanied by Lord Haddington's grandchild, I enjoyed another concert in the same hall as on the previous evening. The programme this time consisted of a Mozart Violin Concerto and Mahler's *Das Lied von der Erde*.

On the following morning, Lord Haddington showed me his garden with its profusion of beautiful flowers, and part of his estate. To call it an estate does not convey its size. It was huge, covering about seventy per cent of the area bounded by the Yamanote line in Tokyo. At lunch, students of Edinburgh University, known to Lord Haddington, joined us for a barbeque at a log cabin-type cottage by the sea. That evening I put on a dinner-jacket (tuxedo in Japanese) and went again to Edinburgh castle to see the military tattoo. Various spectacular events were put on in the square in front of the castle. I was particularly impressed by the performance of the bagpipers. A single piper suddenly appeared at the highest point on Edinburgh castle and in the silence which followed we heard the sound of the bagpipes. It was a phantasmic scene.

On the following day, the 31st, I went to Scone Palace in Perthshire, the home of Lord Mansfield, where I was received by the Earl and Countess of Mansfield and their two children. I was shown around inside the palace by Lady Mansfield who spoke with much good humour and elegance and explained everything in an easily understandable way. Among the many historical objects in the house she showed me was a tree-planting spade, which my parents had used during their visit to Scone Palace in 1976. I could imagine how much they had enjoyed their few days with the Mansfields. Lord Mansfield was a Minister for Northern Ireland when I came to study at Oxford. If he had not had this post I would probably have had my 'home-stay' before going up to Oxford with the Mansfields. Although I only had half a day including lunch with the Mansfields at Scone Palace, thanks to the warm reception they gave me, I had a most relaxing and enjoyable time. In the evening, I went back to the Haddingtons and putting on a dinner-jacket attended a formal dinner. After dinner there was more Scottish dancing and Scottish songs were sung with Haddington's grandchild playing the flute and Counsellor Fuji playing the piano. I remember especially the singing of *Loch Lomond*. At the end, all present joined arms and sang *Auld Lang Syne*.[7] The last night at the Haddingtons was a lively and nostalgic one.

During my three days with the Haddingtons the Earl and his wife, despite the fact that they were getting on in years, accompanied me everywhere and their son and grandson did all they could to entertain me. During my short stay in Scotland I was overwhelmed by the hospitality of my hosts, including the Mansfields. On 1 September, full of fond memories, I left the Haddingtons and went on by car to the Lake District in the North of England. As we came nearer to our destination we were increasingly surrounded by hills. I had not felt deprived of anything while staying with the Halls, but the generally flat landscape made me long for the mountains. I was not 'homesick' but rather 'mountain-sick'. On this trip to Scotland I had not been into the Highlands with their many mountains, but the Lake District, combining both lakes and mountains, cured my 'mountainsickness' and a night in a hotel by a lake provided a chance to rest and relax. That evening perhaps I was too much affected by once more being in the mountains: at any rate, when I was in the corridor after leaving my room, I suddenly realized I had left my key behind. I faced the distressing situation that I was locked out, but I managed to find the manager and borrowed the master key. One could say that this was an extension of my practical language lessons with Mr and Mrs Corcos. Next day, we went round various lakes and visited Wordsworth's cottage. This brought to a close my tour of Scotland and the Lake District and I returned to Oxford by train from Lancaster.

Last month at the Halls

With the arrival of September the days gradually got shorter and there was a feeling of autumn in the air. I only had another month with the Halls. The flowers, which had been blooming in profusion when I had arrived, were getting fewer and the days became quite

---

[7] *Hotaru no hikari* (light of the fireflies) in Japanese.

chilly. The pace of my lessons in English quickened and became more difficult, but I clearly needed a good knowledge of English to pursue my studies and live a full life at Oxford. So I studied as hard as I could. During the month, as part of my education, in addition to studying English, I was given the opportunity of seeing how English justice worked through a visit to the Royal Courts of Justice in Oxford. I also went to Stratford-on-Avon to see Shakespeare's *Henry VIII*.

Colonel Hall and Mr and Mrs Corcos accompanied me to the Royal Courts of Justice. After a chat with the judge I went into the court-room. I was fortunate enough to be seated beside the judge and was able to see from beginning to end part of a case involving arson. The black robes and wig of the judge made me realize that the old traditions were still being maintained. There were many points in the case and in the defence which I had difficulty in following, but it was a good experience to be able to see how the court operated and I found it a valuable addition to my studies.

Mr and Mrs Corcos accompanied me to Stratford-upon-Avon. Among the many Tudor houses in the town we visited the house where Shakespeare was born and the church where he was buried. We then went to the Royal Shakespeare Theatre. Fortunately, as I had studied a summary of the play with Mr and Mrs Corcos, I was able to follow the plot but the play was long and gloomy. I was greatly moved by being able for the first time to visit Shakespeare country and see one of his plays in his home town.

When I look back on my three-month stay with the Halls I think that my experiences can be divided into four important elements. The first element consisted of language study. While I still felt that English was really difficult to learn and had many depths, I thought that in the time since I had first come to stay with the Halls it had become much easier for me to converse in English as well as to read and write English. I owe this to the help I received from Mr and Mrs Corcos and everyone in the Hall household. The second element consisted in meeting all sorts of people not only in the Hall household but also outside. I learnt a good deal from the hospitality which I received about how to entertain and give pleasure to other people. This will be very useful for me in future in entertaining others. The third element is related to the second. I began to have a better understanding of English life as a result of living with the Halls and visiting other houses. The fourth element lay in learning to enjoy country life. I was told that the dream of every Englishman and woman was to be able to live in the country. As circumstances allowed they would try to leave the city for the country where they might do a bit of farming and with their livestock pass the time in peace and tranquillity.

Soon after I arrived to live with the Halls I suffered from hay fever for the first time in my life. Taking meals in the open air and wandering around farms caused slight discomfort. Then when I thought that my hay fever was getting better my nose would be afflicted by the smell of manure. When I first mentioned this to Mrs Corcos she dismissed it with the words 'good country smell' and as I got used to it I also decided that it was a good thing. Because we lived in the country I was able to enjoy the fresh vegetables and jam from the Halls' farm and breathe good country air in such green and pleasant surroundings. I cannot find a better expression than to say that my three months with the Halls was a very peaceful time. I am deeply grateful to the Halls for receiving me so warmly into their home and the happy memories I have from this time.

My stay with the Halls ended on 3 October and in preparation for entering Merton on the following day I moved to Counsellor Fuji's house outside Oxford. Counsellor Fuji's house was an old rectory which he had rented for two years not far from Abingdon in the village of Besselsleigh. Fuji lived here with his wife, two children and niece and did various work connected with my stay at Oxford. I should explain that Counsellor Fuji had been chamberlain to the Shōwa Emperor and Empress since 1970 and had studied at Copenhagen University in Denmark. He had obtained his doctorate for a study of sea urchins and was an expert Viola player. In this connection he served as Vice-Chairman of the Viola Study Association. Fuji had had much experience of living abroad but this was the first time his wife and children had experienced such a lengthy stay overseas. I greatly appreciated the fact that they had so readily accepted this appointment.

Fuji's house was a two-storey simple building. Behind it there was a square-shaped garden of about the size of four tennis courts. which looked out on to farmland. The dining-room and sitting-room, with fireplaces, led off the entrance hall; at the back there was a room with a piano, which could be used as a music room. My room was upstairs at the back with a view of the garden. I used to stay here from time to time after I had entered college, for instance, during vacations and when the college was shut for conferences or other events. It was a very comfortable residence. I was nervous that night before I entered college but I felt at home in the congenial company of the Fujis.

CHAPTER 3

ENTERING OXFORD

———————□———————

Arrival at Merton

On 4 October I left Counsellor Fuji's house to spend two years at Merton; my feelings were a mixture of anticipation and anxiety about the new life I was beginning. Perhaps it was due to the nervousness which I felt, but the brief fifteen minutes it took by car from the Fujis' house, where I had slept the previous night, to Merton seemed particularly long. The sounds of the vehicles passing along the cobbled streets, which always used to please me, sounded oppressive that day.

Sir Rex Richards, the warden, whom I had already met during my stay in London, was there to greet me in front of the college gates. I was immediately asked, as is the custom at Oxford, to sign the register of new students which was presented to me at the porter's lodge. I was so nervous that my hand holding the pen shook and when I wrote my name Naruhito in roman letters my writing looked quite awful. This was the first official action of my stay at Oxford.

Having signed the register and received the key of my room the warden introduced me to two other students. One of them was the chairman of the Middle Common Room to which, as a graduate student, I would belong. The other was the chairman of the Junior Common Room, to which undergraduates belong. The chairman of the Middle Common Room was an American called J. He was tall and, at close range, his face, on which a magnificent beard sprouted, looked rather off-putting. He was a very gloomy-looking person, but his eyes showed that he was also gentle and kind. On the other hand, the chairman of the Junior Common Room was an English girl called M who had a very pretty face.

In the Front Quad I met representatives of the English and Japanese media. I was asked various questions by the representative of a local radio station, but the only question I can now remember was 'Do you want to join in all student activities including going to the pub?' I replied in words which I intended to mean that I probably would want to do so. Sir Rex interposed and said: 'As the Prince has only just arrived and is nervous, the questioning should now stop' and the meeting with the media was brought to a close. At that time I really was anxious about the life that lay ahead of me and about what I could do while I was at Oxford. I simply did not have enough ability in English at that time to explain how I then felt.

Carrying a suitcase I made my way up the stone stairs to my rooms on the second floor which was the top floor. My rooms were at the end and consisted of two adjoining rooms, a study and a bedroom. My bathroom lay across a different corridor on which was the room for my police guard. That corridor led to the small second floor landing, and had a door which was closed at night. From my study which was the size of about eight *tatami* mats[1] I had the view which I had hoped for – south over Christ Church Meadow, while from my bedroom I could look down on the peaceful garden of the college. With such a good and quiet outlook I could not have had a better set of rooms.

My desk was big enough to provide ample space for any number of papers. Within easy reach of my desk there was a wooden revolving bookstand and facing the desk there was a bookcase with three shelves. The top of the bookcase was too high for me to reach, but the bookcase by my desk and the revolving bookstand were within easy reach when I was studying, as I could take up any book I wanted without having to move round too far. There were chairs and a table

---

[1] *Tatami*, which are mats made of straw, usually measure about 6.0 x 3.0 feet, but the size varies slightly in different parts of Japan. They are about 2.4 inches thick. Room sizes in Japan are usually described as consisting of a given number of *tatami* mats.

in the middle of the room and a sofa by the wall. In addition, there were two upright armchairs by the door and an electric fire. In the bedroom, apart from the bed, there was a wardrobe; adjoining this was a wash-basin which had doors to it so that it could be closed off from the rest of the room when not in use. There was also a chest of drawers with three large drawers. And the window above the bed had a curtain so unreliably flimsy it looked as if it would tear at any minute.

It was good to have rooms which I could use as I wanted. I only had one suitcase but I spent some time deciding by trial and error where to put my various things. The light fades early in England in October and by the time I had set my things out it was already getting dark.

Shortly afterwards, as I had promised J, I went down to the bar. Attracted by the smell of beer I soon found myself in the bar and was greeted in the dingy light by a number of curious students. I joined J and M at a table in the middle of the room and some students gathered round. The first girl, to whom I was introduced, was wearing a straw hat, despite the fact that we were indoors, and had a silver star on her forehead. I wondered what sort of a strange place I had come to. So I was relieved to see that some of the others were typical undergraduates such as I had imagined them to be. I can still remember that it was at this moment sitting in the midst of the aroma of the beer and watching the forms and gestures of the students in the gloom that I realized I was in Oxford so far away across the sea.

Invited by J to accompany him I went into hall for my first meal in college. Helping myself to soup and a meat dish at the door we took our seats. J sat opposite me at the long, old and worn dining-table. The benches we sat on were uncomfortable. Looking round, all I could see in the darkness were the faces of the students lit up by the lamps set on the tables. Each had different features and different coloured hair. It was all something I was seeing for the very first time. An enormous number of portraits of people I did not know hung on the walls around the hall. Above was almost total darkness, but I could just make out the shape of the beams in the dizzyingly high ceiling. J, guessing that I was feeling overwhelmed by the atmosphere, assumed an especially kind expression. It was a flurried meal.

In my confusion I have forgotten whether I drank the soup and ate the meat and do not remember anything about the conversation. All I recall is that I gave a sigh of relief when the meal, which was better than I had expected, was all over.

Once again, J said, 'Let's go and have our coffee in a friend's room' and so we went up another stone staircase in a different part of the college. The occupant of the room was a girl who was a friend of M's rather than of J's. The room was much the same size as mine, but as there was a bed in the room I realized that it must be a combined bedroom and living-room. A number of others came in including the girl with the silver mark on her forehead. There clearly were not enough chairs to go round. So the newcomers sat on the carpet. As I was standing there with a blank look on my face I was offered a chair that looked as if it was ready to collapse. We chatted sitting in a circle and mugs of coffee were handed round; everyone spoke freely. Unfortunately, while I understood that they were chatting about the joys and troubles of student life I had no opportunity to contribute to the conversation. But I began to understand how they spent their time after dinner and I was happy just to be there. This was also the first time I saw my fellow students nonchalantly putting their mugs on the floor.

In this way my first day at Merton came to a close. Saying goodbye to all present I returned to my room and prepared for bed. I buried myself beneath my three blankets. It was a quiet night and I did not hear a sound from anywhere round about.

Before matriculation

My life at Merton really started from the following day. To get from my room to hall I had a few minutes walk as this was in a different building. Despite the fact that it was only early October it felt chilly that first morning at Merton. This was the second time I had been in hall. I was surprised to see how different it looked in the morning light. One reason for this was the small number of students there, but I was again astonished by the fine beams criss-crossing in the high ceiling. I was rather afraid that it would be cold in hall in winter.

Although I had joined the college this did not mean that the formalities for entering the university would follow immediately. The university entrance ceremony did not take place until 15 October. Before that there were various college and university ceremonies to be held. On the morning of the 6th I put in an appearance at a meeting in the JCR to which I had been invited. In the afternoon J invited various members of the MCR including myself to tea in his room and I went along. They seemed a very nice group of students. One student, who wore glasses and had a beard, seemed particularly voluble. While holding pieces of cake we began to introduce ourselves and spoke about what we were planning to do. Looking back now I realize that most of those I met at tea that day were the ones with whom I developed particularly friendly relations during my two years at Oxford. This tea turned out to be an unexpected opportunity to meet new people.

That evening there was a college admission ceremony in hall. The new students entered hall one by one as their names were called out. After greeting the warden we entered our names in the register. This was a very brief ceremony but the atmosphere was most congenial. Afterwards, there was a dinner to welcome the new students, attended by various senior students and members of the teaching staff of the college. I was placed next to Dr Highfield. I had already met him and greatly enjoyed the dinner. At the end of the meal Sir Rex Richards, the warden, struck the table with a mallet and gave a short speech to close the ceremony mentioning that we should not keep the domestic staff too long. I felt that I was now really a member of the college.

On the 7th we were given general advice about things we needed to know about college life, such as how to get in touch with the doctor responsible for treating members of the college, and other important points to note. After listening to these instructions we moved to the Examinations Schools building, where exams took place as well as lectures, and were given an introduction to the club activities in the University as a whole. I was surprised by the variety; there were so many different facilities including sports clubs, the union where debates took place, cultural circles as well as places where we could enjoy meals. In the evening, I attended a party in the

MCR to welcome newcomers to the college. I was impressed by the way the students were able to relax and mix freely and how they were good at socializing. Here I was able to find many valuable friends.

There were no particular ceremonies on the 8th and I went to a cinema in the town to see the film *Gandhi* directed by Richard Attenborough. It was a long but well-produced film and faithfully reflected Gandhi's philosophy and desire for peace. At the end of the film, the fact that more than half the audience did not immediately get up to go attested to its excellence.

In the morning of the 9th there was a lecture by Dr Highfield about the history of the college, which was attended, as I remember, by a large number of new students. This was followed by a mini-tour to see the places he had mentioned. In the evening I was invited to a party of the Oxford Music Society probably because they knew that I played the viola.

In the afternoon of the 10th I attended a history seminar. Professor Howard's lecture to students, who were going to study history, was relatively easy to follow. In the evening, I took part in a drinks party to welcome new students to Merton where I had the good fortune to be able to talk with members of the teaching and college staff. I went on to a party for students particularly interested in the history of the college. This was a good chance to meet other students and a most enjoyable party, but I was in some difficulties because, when I was asked about my particular field of research, I could not answer as I had not yet decided what this would be.

My first week in Oxford thus came to an end with a round of parties. I think they were very relevant for my future time at Merton. I met a large number of students at these parties which were not just occasions for drinking and boisterousness. The prime purpose of these important social occasions was to enable people to meet others and converse informally with a glass in one hand. We Japanese tend to get together in groups of people we already have connections with. I did not see that sort of thing at Oxford. I felt that everyone was delighted to talk and exchange views with anyone. As for dress, people either dressed informally or, surprisingly frequently, put on dinner-jackets. While I was at Oxford I always had a dinner-jacket ready in my room.

There are all sorts of parties, as I once found to my chagrin. It was after the entrance ceremony. I thought that parties always involved a meal, so I did not have any supper before going to an evening party where there was nothing to eat except crisps and nibbles!

University Entrance ceremony

The 15th, the day of the university entrance ceremony, soon came round. It was a really chilly day with light drizzle. At nine o'clock the new entrants to the college met in the front quad. My name was first called out as 'Mr Naruhito'. This was greeted with a burst of laughter from the other students and my name was corrected to 'Prince Naruhito'. The stiff atmosphere relaxed and having replied 'yes' to my name I went along with the other new entrants to the Sheldonian Theatre where the ceremony was to be held. It was arranged that while I was at Oxford I would simply be called 'Hiro' by staff and fellow students. I thought that 'Hiro' was much easier for people to remember than 'Naruhito' and I liked the sound of 'Hiro' as a name.

Since I had already joined Merton and started going to lectures, some readers may wonder what was meant by the term 'entrance ceremony'. The ceremony that day was actually the 'Matriculation Ceremony' where the term 'matriculate' means permission to enter the university. Dress on this occasion for men consisted of a white shirt, white bow tie and suit under a black gown (which was actually a simple piece of black cloth with holes for the arms) which was also worn on other ceremonial occasions and at formal meals, with a mortar board on the head. This is similar to the headgear of students at Waseda University without the brim. The gowns worn by graduate students, which hang down below the hips, are longer than those worn by undergraduates, which only stretch as far as the hips. Women students wore white blouses with a black ribbon and a gown on top. Led by a representative of the college we began a procession to the place where the ceremony was to be held. We passed along the cobbled pavement of Merton Street into the narrow High Street and across over Radcliffe Square into the Sheldonian Theatre. Fortunately, an English girl who was studying Japanese and a young student from the Philippines whom I had met soon after entering

Merton were walking comparatively near me and there was another English student in our group who took it upon himself to look after me. As we passed in front of the Japanese camera crews I shall not forget his face as he said the single word 'Smile!'

As I walked through the medieval-looking streets of modern Oxford, wearing a gown and a white bow tie, I thought I am really now an Oxford man. Simply taking part in the procession to the Sheldonian theatre made it a memorable day for me, but the ceremonies inside the hall were overwhelming. The beautiful round theatre had been designed by the famous English architect Sir Christopher Wren who also designed St Paul's Cathedral in London. Apart from matriculation ceremonies the theatre was used for the conferment of degrees. The proceedings began at 9.45 with solemn music played on the organ. Latin was the language used throughout and the only words I understood were 'sit down, please' which were said by the vice-chancellor in English. I followed the ceremony by reading the translation on the leaflet which I had in my hand. During the ceremony the persons who had led us from our colleges declared 'We introduce our students to the University'. To this the vice-chancellor responded formally: 'Everyone of you should be conscious of the great expectations placed on you by the community and the nation and the hope that you will study hard, as hard as you can, while you are here.' The ceremony lasted a mere fifteen minutes, but it made me realize the weight of tradition here in Oxford. I was relieved that I could now regard myself as a member of the university.

CHAPTER 4

ABOUT OXFORD

————————□————————

'Dreaming spires'[1]

I should like to give a brief introduction to Oxford. The modern city of Oxford has a population of over 100,000. It lies some ninety kilometres to the northwest of London on the middle reaches of the Thames. The name Oxford derives from the two words 'ox' and 'ford' meaning a river which an ox could walk across. In England there are many place names ending in 'ford' such as Stratford and Bradford where there were shallow places at which a river could be crossed fairly easily. The Oxford crest naturally shows an ox crossing a river. The centre of Oxford and the main street in the city is the High Street which runs east to west. The main buildings of the city are ranged on either side of the High Street to the north and south.

In the north of this central area are St Mary's Church, All Souls, Queen's, Brasenose and a number of other colleges as well as the Bodleian Library and its annex Radcliffe Camera. To the north and facing on to Broad Street is the Sheldonian Theatre while on the south side of the High Street are University College and Oriel together with shops and restaurants. Going west from the High Street you come to Carfax crossroads which is the busiest spot in Oxford. Turning north you then come to the Cornmarket which is a shopping street: if you turn south you come into St Aldate's street

---

[1] From Mathew Arnold's poem *Thyrsis*: 'And that sweet City with her dreaming spires, She needs not June for beauty's heightening.'

where you can see the tower of Christ Church. Going further south you reach a bridge over the Thames. Suburbs of the city lie south of the river and of Christ Church Meadow which is a large field by the river. To the north there are various green spaces including University Park while to the east is the Cherwell, a branch of the Thames, which flows under a bridge by the side of Magdalen.

For a view of the city in its entirety you should go towards Headington and South Park in the north-east of the city and climb the gentle green slope. The old college buildings, churches and towers will appear one by one as you look back. While I was studying at Oxford I went many times to this spot and enjoyed the view. It was best towards sunset. I can never forget the moment when silhouettes of the spires of Oxford one by one caught the evening light and seemed to float above the mists. This mystical sight, which has aroused so much admiration, is called Oxford's 'Dreaming Spires'. Going on from South Park down a gentle slope you soon come to a junction where there is a dual carriageway to the left, but if you go straight on to the right you will see the spire of Madgalen College Chapel which seems to mark the entrance to Oxford. Passing by Magdalen there is a slight curve in the High Street and Queen's, All Souls, St Mary's Church and other ancient buildings of the University appear one by one in a really dramatic way. If you are lucky you will see some students in their gowns among the throng walking up and down the High Street. The term 'town and gown' means the citizens of Oxford and the university students.

'Town and Gown' – a brief history of Oxford University

It is not entirely clear why a university was established at Oxford. According to a leading source, in the twelfth century King Henry II banished Thomas à Becket, the Archbishop of Canterbury, to the continent and in order to prevent contacts between the Archbishop and English students studying at the University of Paris, King Henry summoned the students to return home. The students who came home and other students who were unable to pursue their studies at Paris took up their abode in Oxford and the university was born. It is not clear when the university was formally established, but documents have been preserved which show that soon after 1100 there were students at Oxford and it is said that up to about 1300 Oxford had some 1,500 students. Oxford was probably chosen because it was a place where routes crossed in the centre of England and it was easy for people to congregate there. There are not many documents which describe what Oxford University was like in those early days and such accounts, as there are, are not necessarily accurate, but it seems that the teachers and students lived in rooms which they rented from local people and that teaching was carried out in the teachers' rooms, in churches or in the cloisters of monasteries. In the Middle Ages a university was where teachers and students lived a communal life. It did not have to have buildings of its own.

For this reason, and when from time to time students did not pay their rent, petty quarrels occurred between students and townsfolk and sometimes led to brawls when weapons were used on both sides. This was the origin of the popular term 'town and gown'. In 1209 when one student wounded and killed an Oxford woman the trouble led to a court case and the university was forced to close. Many students and teachers left the town and, it is said, moved to Cambridge, leading to the beginning of the university there.

The antagonism between town and gown was at its most violent in 1355. The disturbance in that year was said to have resulted from a row caused by several students over the quality and stinginess of the wine served in *Swyndlestock Tavern* in the centre of town. The citizens and the students gathered respectively in the neighbourhood of St Martin's Church in the area of Carfax and in St Mary's Church. The disturbances lasted two days and resulted in many dead and wounded. The incident was brought to an end by the expulsion of the students from the city. The university used this occasion to petition the king and request the strengthening of their privileges while the town had to pay compensation to those injured.

As an aside, I might add that I was advised to avoid going out alone at night in town wearing a gown. I was surprised to discover that the antagonism between town and gown still lingers to this day.

In order to stop these quarrels a number of students got together to rent a house and thus began the system whereby the students selected their own leader and began to live in a community of their own. The houses, which were called 'halls', were granted legal status by clerics, aristocrats and others and became colleges.

I think many readers will know that in the Middle Ages university scholars had a special status as members of a guild. At that time students spent seven years living together as pupils under a chief whom they called 'master' in the same way as craftsmen served as apprentices under masters in their trade. Relics of these practices can be seen from the use of the terms 'master', 'doctor', and 'professor'. The word 'masterpiece' originates from an apprentice making a work of art in order to become a 'master'.

When walking around Oxford one occasionally met tourists who asked: 'Where is the University?' It was not only Japanese who were puzzled in this way. The question can be said to reflect a special feature of Oxford. There is no single building which can be described as 'Oxford University': there are thirty-five colleges in Oxford today, including four colleges[2] which only take women and seven which are for postgraduates and research students. These are all independent institutions but together they form Oxford University. The head of the University is the Chancellor, but this is an honorary post and responsibility for the administration of the university falls to the vice-chancellor. While I was at Oxford the Chancellor was former Prime Minister Harold Macmillan who had become the Earl of Stockton. Like the departments in Japanese universities Oxford has various faculties and students invariably belong both to a college and to a faculty. I belonged to the Faculty of Modern History. While I was at Oxford there were some 12,400 students (7,600 men and 4,800 women) in the university, including 1,850 overseas students.

College system

Any account of Oxford University must cover the college system. Let me explain briefly the special characteristics of the system. Colleges are in essence places where students studying different

---

[2] Now two,

subjects live a communal life together. Some colleges are exclusively for women, but most colleges take both men and women. Women were only admitted to Oxford comparatively recently. The largest colleges have some 500 students and the smaller ones about 150. The colleges are of all sizes but the average number of students in any one college is about 300. In the average college, in addition to the students' rooms, there are usually a chapel, library, dining-hall, office, common-room, teachers' rooms and bar. Undergraduates should in principle live within a radius of six miles of Carfax and graduate students within a radius of twelve miles. As a result, students either rent a flat in the city or live in college. At Merton, of which I was a member, there were some 300 students, half of whom lived in college. It was obligatory for undergraduates to spend the first year of their three-year degree course in college.

Colleges are administered by the head of the college and the fellows. The colleges use different titles for their head. Merton, for instance, is headed by a warden, Balliol by a master, Exeter by a rector, Magdalen by a president, Worcester by a provost, Brasenose by a principal. The fellows who are teachers and researchers are informally referred to as 'dons'. One of the fellows in charge of the accounts is the bursar; internal administration comes under the domestic bursar, finance under the financial bursar and college property under the estates bursar. It may be surprising to speak of college estates, but in fact many colleges own large areas of land and are accordingly landed proprietors. Scouts, who are college servants, clean the rooms except at weekends. According to college gossip, they also keep their eyes and ears open and observe what is going on in the students' lives, checking for instance whether someone of the opposite sex is staying in a room and that rooms are tidy and being used for their proper purpose.

The college system is said to have been started around the thirteenth century. There is still some dispute about which is the oldest college – Merton, University College or Balliol. Merton was the first college to receive its charter in 1264 (University College received its charter in 1280 and Balliol in 1284). Merton has some of the oldest buildings still in use; one part goes back to the end of the thirteenth century. University College is said by some to have been founded by

King Alfred the Great, in the ninth century, but there is no documentary proof of this, although it is known for a fact that in 1249 William of Durham supplied funds to provide for a large number of students. There is no doubt that these funds were increased and became attached to the college, although it is not clear whether a college existed at that time. There are records which show that in 1266 a number of scholars got together under John de Balliol; on this basis Balliol College claims that it dates back to 1263. On the basis of the date on which it received its charter and on having the oldest extant buildings in Oxford, Merton is the oldest of all the colleges. University College was the first to receive a financial donation and Balliol was the first college known to have scholars. It is not easy to reach a conclusion on this issue; we need to consider not only the various formal documents but also the actual facts and to take note of the way in which the colleges have grown over the years, but we can say that colleges had been established by the thirteenth century. Exeter, Oriel and Queen's were established in the fourteenth century. The establishment of New College needs to be dealt with separately.

In 1379 the bishop responsible for the University was William of Wykeham. He established New College near the north wall of the city with the aim of educating candidates for the clergy whose numbers had been greatly decreased by the plague which had been prevailing at that time. The adjective 'new' in New College does not just indicate that as compared with existing colleges it was new; it applied to various other aspects of the college. For example the college plan provided for the first time for a quadrangle (called 'quad' in Oxford and 'court' in Cambridge). Generally speaking at Oxford the quad consists of a square garden covered in grass and surrounded by buildings. The oldest quad in Oxford is claimed to be 'Mob Quad' in Merton. This was by chance a square. In the case of New College the quad, designed by William of Wykeham himself, is surrounded by the main buildings of the college, namely the chapel, the library, the lodging for the head of the college and the fellows' rooms. This was the first purpose-built quad in Oxford and it became the pattern for other colleges founded later. New College had more fellows and larger buildings than any of the colleges established previously. In educational terms the college did not confine itself to the education of graduates who already had a master's degree but also took in undergraduates who were to live in college with the fellows. As I explain below this was the beginning of the unique tutorial system. In these ways New College had a major impact on the development of later colleges.

In the fifteenth century three additional colleges were established. These were Lincoln, All Souls and Magdalen. All Souls was established solely for research and is different from every other college in Oxford in that it does not cater for any undergraduates.

I cannot comment further here on every college, but here is a list of the other later colleges in the order of their foundation: sixteenth century: Brasenose, Corpus Christi, Christchurch, Trinity, St John's; seventeenth century: Wadham and Pembroke; nineteenth century and later: Keble, Manchester, Somerville and others.

As I have explained, Oxford consists of numerous colleges with some dating back to the thirteenth century. Many have historically interesting buildings. Sadly, many of these were remodelled in the Victorian era, but some still remain as they were. I think that the college system lies at the heart of Oxford University's educational philosophy.

Education at Oxford and regular activities in the University

I do not have space to enumerate here all the reasons why I consider Oxford's education so excellent. I shall refer to some of these below but I should like to mention in particular the tutorial system (called at Cambridge 'supervision'). The tutorial system means the teaching on a one-to-one basis by a teacher who has been appointed to look after a pupil who meets with his tutor once a week. The student presents for discussion an essay which he has prepared and lists problems he has encountered in his research. The tutorial lasts about an hour during which the tutor sets the theme of the essay to be prepared for the following week's session and gives the student a list of books and documents to be consulted in its preparation. This is generally very long and more than anyone can absorb in the time available. Depending on the individual student he may be asked to join in a tutorial for another student; he may also have two tutorials in one week if he is studying two different subjects. Graduate students generally have two supervisors, one within the college and one outside. In my case the tutor with whom I had one-to-one sessions was Professor Mathias of All Souls and the thesis I wrote while at Oxford was assessed by him.

My tutor within Merton was Dr Highfield. He helped me with the essays which Professor Mathias asked me to prepare and I was able to discuss with him any problems which cropped up in my research. Dr Highfield's position was that of 'moral tutor' or 'in college tutor'. He acted essentially as a tutor in the same way as Professor Mathias and to distinguish them I called the latter my supervisor. The role of a tutor is primarily to give guidance in study and research, but the tutor is also available to give advice on any problems or stress that the student may encounter. The experience of studying and living together promotes mutual understanding and respect and leads to the development of close relationships. This system of close contacts between pupils and teachers encourages students to develop opinions of their own and is an excellent way of training them to construct logical arguments, although some people think that the views of teachers are too strongly reflected in the opinions of students.

According to the book entitled *Igirisu Shakaikeizaishi no tabi* (A journey through English Social Economic History) by Ugawa Kaoru, the tutorial system developed from the building of rooms intended for both study and living. Thus, at New College, which was established in the fourteenth century, large rooms were built in which four students were to study and live together. The eldest of the four was responsible for supervising the study of the other three. This is said to have been the origin of the system of individual tuition in English universities.

The tutorial system has an important role in education at Oxford. Lectures are primarily an aide to the preparation of essays for tutorials. For a student reading history as a main subject lectures lasting an hour began at 9.0 in the morning while seminars generally took place in the afternoon from 5.0 or later.

I shall now comment briefly on Oxford University activities. Every year there are three university terms lasting eight weeks.

The first term, called Michaelmas term starts in early October. As I have explained, the first ceremony of the term is that of matriculation. The actual day on which the ceremony takes place varies from year to year. When I went to Oxford the ceremony was held on 15 October. In addition, at the beginning of the academic year, all the university clubs and associations organize introductory parties to welcome new members. The first term ends in the middle of December. During the vacation the college may be used for conferences and other purposes and undergraduates have to vacate their rooms. Graduate students depending on the nature of their research can generally make arrangements to stay in college and many do so.

The second term, called Hilary, lasts from mid-January to the end of March. I do not recall any particular ceremonies during this term, but around the end of the term the Oxford and Cambridge boat race takes place on the Thames and attracts a great deal of attention. The race is watched by crowds lining the river bank and is broadcast on television. (See chapter below on sports.)

The third term, called Trinity, lasts from the end of March to roughly the end of June. The weather is better during this period and this is the season for all sorts of sports and outside activities. At 6.0 o'clock on the first of May the choir climbs up to the top of Magdalen tower and the ceremony of singing 'May Morning' takes place. Despite the early hour large numbers collect on Magdalen Bridge from where the tower can be seen. This ceremony is said to date back to the early sixteenth century. Perhaps because it was still rather dark and chilly and I was quite sleepy the voices gave me a mystical feeling. The pubs were allowed to open at this early hour on this day and after I had listened to the song I went with friends, who had come out with me, and enjoyed an early glass of beer at a pub.

In June, I recall the good weather when I could see students lying down on the college lawn reading books, and chatting. This was the time when all sorts of sports competitions, especially in rowing, were held between the colleges. I was fortunate enough to be chosen as one of the college tennis team and was able to join in competitions with other colleges every week.

In May, popular dance parties called 'May Balls', a special feature of Oxford, take place. Students who usually wore jeans all the time would dress up in dinner-jackets and go to the balls with their partners in evening dress and other finery. Not all colleges had May Balls, but Merton's was very popular; it began about 10.0 o'clock and went on until about 6.0 the following morning. One problem was the rather high price of the tickets. In the course of the evening supper was served. A lot went on; a jazz band and a string quartet provided music, there was a disco and there were jugglers and other performers. This ball came at the end of Trinity Term which marked the end of the academic year; the undergraduates then left Oxford and the university had a long four month vacation.

Merton

I have referred quite often to Merton but I should like to add a brief guide to the college. Merton was founded in 1264 in the middle of the thirteenth century by the Lord Chancellor Walter de Merton, later Bishop of Rochester. The college has had a chequered history since its foundation. It was a Royalist centre during the puritan revolution in the seventeenth century when Charles I was executed. The college today contains a room reputed to have been used by Queen Henrietta Maria, consort of Charles I. While the Queen was taking refuge in Merton the King lived in Christ Church. According to one story, in those days Merton and Christ Church were connected by an underground passage-way. At the time of the puritan revolution one of the few natural scientists was appointed at the King's request to be warden of the college. He was William Harvey (1578–1657) who discovered the principles governing the circulation of the blood. In later years, two other doctors of medicine held the post of warden. While I was at Merton the warden, Sir Rex Richards, was a chemistry scholar and I was surprised to hear that he was the first warden since 1750 to have been a scientist.[3]

Based on the map overleaf let us take a walk round the college. The college faces the cobbled Merton Street. Going in through the gateway you come to the relatively broad front quad. Standing in the corner you willl see ahead of you the dining hall, and looming

---

[3] In recent years scientists have often replaced theologians and classicists as heads of colleges.

MERTON COLLEGE, OXFORD

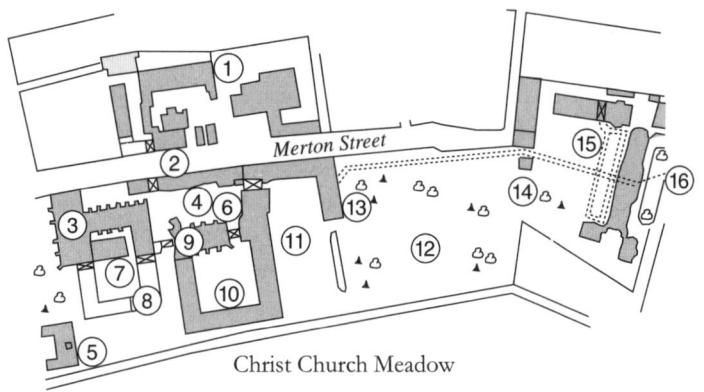

1. Real Tennis Court	9. Hall
2. Main Gate	10. Fellows' Quad
3. Chapel	11. St Alban's Quad
4. Porter's lodge	12. Fellows' garden
5. Grove	13. My rooms
6. Front Quad	14. Summer House
7. Mob Quad	15. Warden's residence
8. Library	16. Rose Lane

large to the right Merton College Chapel, while to the left you can see the entrance to the fellows' quad. The dining hall was built in the latter part of the thirteenth century but most of it was rebuilt in the late eighteenth and nineteenth centuries. Part of the massive iron entrance door to the hall with its convoluted decoration is said to date from the time when the college was established. The fellows' quad was put up at the beginning of the seventeenth century when Henry Savile was the warden; this was the first quad in Oxford to have three-storey buildings. Crossing the front quad and moving left you come to the undergraduates' rooms in St Alban's Quad.

The undergraduates' rooms and the library are next to the chapel. Passing through the narrow passage between the chapel and the hall you come immediately to Mob Quad. As I have already explained, this is the oldest quad in Oxford. By chance, I got to know a student who had a room in one corner of Mob Quad. When I visited his

42

room I found that the windows were small and the room was rather dark. The walls had an ancient medieval appearance and I felt that I was back in olden times. The library on the first floor, which even today suggests its fourteenth century origins, is one of the oldest in England. Among its many important treasures is the first printed version of the bible in Welsh. A particularly interesting item is a chained book. This dates from the Middle Ages when books were sometimes attached to chains to prevent them from being stolen. At Merton, until the end of the sixteenth century, important and rare books were attached to chains and placed on desks between the windows. These books and a number of books in the library, which were passed on to the library by fellows of the college, are part of the college's inheritance. As a result of the purchase at the end of the sixteenth century of a quantity of printed books the number of desks in the library was no longer sufficient and the first staffed library in England was created. I understand that the custom of chaining books lasted in Oxford until the end of the eighteenth century. It is said that a ghost may appear in the library, but I never had a chance of meeting it while I was studying at Merton and the existence of this phantom has not been confirmed.

Going from Mob Quad you soon come to the entrance to the chapel. Parts of the chapel go back to the end of the thirteenth century. An interesting feature of the building is that although it should have had the shape of a cross it lacks the end part of the cross and is thus in the form of a T. According to one theory, the end part could not be built because of shortage of funds. As a result, Merton College Chapel is the first example among Oxford College chapels which is constructed in the shape of a T. In addition to the normal church services concerts were occasionally given in the chapel. Merton's Kodály Choir gives a concert in the chapel once a year. The choir was founded by a pupil of the Hungarian composer Kodály who spent a number of years at Merton and this was how its name originated. In the year I joined the university, perhaps due to the good acoustics and fine singing, I was much moved by the performance of Handel's *Messiah*. The chapel has some rare old stained glass dating from about the fourteenth century with images of various saints; facing them there are a number of images in stained glass of the same person. He is reputed to be the donor of the glass, Maunsfield,[4] who had been Chancellor of the University and who perhaps wanted future generations to see his portrait and be aware of his achievements. There were in all twenty-four images of him. Dr Highfield kindly took me to see the chapel tower built in the middle of the fifteenth century. From the top the view of Oxford was as good as one could wish. However, while going up and down the spiral staircase, my clothes became covered with the dust of ages.

Returning to the front quad and going in the direction of St Alban's quad you see the building containing the students' rooms with the bar for the exclusive use of the JCR in the basement. Especially at dinner time the smell of beer comes wafting out. On the first floor there is the MCR common-room. There is also a room with a large television screen and a so-called games room. Most of those who live in St Alban's quad are students, but there are also some rooms which are used by the teaching staff for tutorials. St Alban's was once an Oxford Hall which became part of Merton at the end of the nineteenth century. This was where I lived while I was at Oxford. This quad is surrounded by buildings on three sides; on the fourth side there is an iron gate through which the college garden can be seen. The ridges of the buildings make them look as though they are all connected, but in fact they are all separate buildings and if you want to go from one to another you have to go down to the ground floor and go outside. Passing from the quad between the buildings you come to the back garden. This is the much beloved Fellows' Garden which has a large fine lawn on which it is tempting to lie down. In good weather the students gather here to chat and enjoy themselves. In the early spring great numbers of crocuses and daffodils spring up as if they are encircling an old tree. The back garden is separated from Christ Church meadow by the medieval city wall marking the southern edge of Oxford. From the wall above the back garden there was a pleasant place provided with a seat from

---

[4] Henry de Maunsfield, also spelt Maunnesfeld, Mammesfeld or Maymysfeld who died in 1328 was a fellow of Merton. He was Chancellor of the University in 1309 and again in 1311. He became Dean of Lincoln in 1316. According to the DNB (OUP, 1997) 'In 1283 ... he filled with glass at his expense all the side windows of the chancel of the old collegiate church of St John the Baptist in Merton College, putting his monogram on several of them.'

which there was a good view of the meadow. In one corner of the garden there was a small and attractive single-storey white music room called the Summer House.

Following the city wall and going towards the west you come to the spot where through an iron gate you can see St Alban's Quad. From here you have a good view of all the buildings around the quad. You can also see from here my rooms on the second floor. Going on from here you pass behind the fellows' quad and come to the south side of Mob Quad and the chapel. This area is called the Grove and there are a number of buildings containing students' rooms. In front behind an iron fence is a narrow road leading to Christ Church meadow. Most readers will probably have heard the name of Irvine, the mountaineer, who disappeared with Mallory in their 1924 climb of Mount Everest. He had been an undergraduate at Merton and had climbed the chapel wall many times. There is a monument to the memory of this mountaineer standing inconspicuously in the Grove as if it symbolizes his death in Mallory's shadow. This takes us to the end of our tour of Merton.

There are also student rooms in the area called Rose Lane to the east next to the botanical garden as well as many outside the college in Holywell Street. When I was at Merton there were, according to the records, which I have by me, 230 undergraduates and 80 graduate students as well as 50 research fellows. About half of the research fellows were teaching fellows who gave tutorials. Candidates wanting to enter Merton were encouraged to take up the study of subjects for which there were specialist tutors at the college. In my time at Merton there was the comparatively large number of twelve students reading modern history. There were seven students in each of the groups reading classics, physics, chemistry and mathematics. There were six reading law, five English, physiology, biochemistry, modern linguistics, and music. Among them were students reading the three subjects of philosophy, politics and economics (commonly referred to as PPE) as well as others reading both history and modern linguistics or history and economics. I shall now move on to write about my life at Oxford.

CHAPTER 5

DAILY LIFE AT OXFORD

————————□————————

In the mornings

My day at Oxford started with breakfast in hall which began at 8.15. There were far fewer students at breakfast in hall than at lunch or dinner. Usually, only around twenty turned up at breakfast so that even if I was a bit late I could easily find a seat and did not have to worry that there would be nothing left. Toast and an egg dish were always on the menu plus, varying from day to day, ham, bacon or sausage etc; it was all self-service. Coffee and tea were, of course, also available. Interestingly, perhaps because of the old religious custom of serving fish on fast days, kippers were served on Fridays. I tried a kipper once but found it difficult to remove the bones and I did not care for the taste. My breakfast generally consisted of a slice of toast, some cereal, such as corn flakes, and tea. When there were boiled eggs on the menu I usually took one. Tea and coffee were obtained from urns by the door. The tea was very strong and the same colour as the coffee. The dining hall was only open for breakfast for half an hour. Anyone who overslept could, however, get a late breakfast from the undergraduates' bar.

After breakfast I used to go to the college office where, if I was in for lunch and dinner, I put my name in the book. If by chance one forgot to do this and was stopped by the steward at the door of the dining hall one was usually allowed in. At dinner on Wednesdays and Fridays Merton students could bring up to three guests and entertain them to dinner in the first floor lobby where the guest table was situated. This was a popular place to dine as the food at the guest table was a good deal better than in hall. On mornings when bookings were taken for the guest table during the following week there was usually a long queue of students wanting to register, but many of them had to put their names on the waiting list. There were, however, generally some cancellations and they might be lucky in securing places.

I would then go and collect my mail and newspaper from my pigeon hole. When I first entered college I had lots of invitations to parties and events as well as letters from people in Britain and abroad. There might be messages from Dr Highfield or Professor Mathias or from other Merton students, some scribbled on scraps of paper. On Valentine's Day there were cards from various unknowns. There were also occasional messages from Japanese tourists who had visited Merton. Among them were some from students who had just graduated from the Gakushūin and who had apparently called at the college during a tour to Europe during the spring vacation. The porters were most assiduous in looking after my mail and as a result I never encountered any problems. Now that I come to think of it my mail box in college was the most important way for me to develop social contacts. Every morning *The Times* was delivered to my mail box. I ordered it from the shop nearest to the college and paid for it in advance. When the newspaper did not appear one day I realized that my subscription must have run out. So I went round to the shop, bought that day's paper and renewed my subscription.

After this I returned to my room and usually drank some coffee while glancing through the newspaper. I had bought a kettle in Oxford after I had joined the university to make hot water for my coffee; it turned itself off automatically once the water had boiled.

Meanwhile, the scout came, removed any rubbish I might have and gave the rooms a simple clean. Once a week she went over the rooms with a vacuum cleaner and some scouts used to chat a lot, too, which I enjoyed. In my first year the scout responsible for my rooms was married to a policeman and was someone the college had specially engaged for me. My second year scout was always startled whenever she inadvertently touched an alarm clock I had brought with me which spoke the time when you touched it. She complained one day that MacDonalds had opened a branch in Oxford and when I said that there was a MacDonalds near the university where I had studied in Tokyo, she expressed great surprise and advised me 'you should do without those sorts of American things!' The scout cleaned the room but did not do the washing which I had to do for myself.

When my scout had left it was time for me to get down to my studies. Some mornings I had lectures to attend or had to collect documents from the library or public record office, but generally I spent the time in my room preparing my essays. Lunch was from 12.45. In addition to Merton students, students from other colleges used to come for lunch; as a result, there tended to be a long queue outside the hall. On particularly crowded days the queue stretched as far as the college office; it was especially cold waiting on winter days, but I practically never saw anyone attempt to jump the queue. As one entered step by step into the hall, one was hit by the warmth inside. At lunch, which was self-service, there was a choice of three or four dishes. One dish might be a meat stew; another might be spaghetti with a meat sauce and a third a meat pie. Having collected a plate for the main dish you held it out in front of you and the person in charge gave you, as you indicated, potatoes and cooked vegetables such as Brussels sprouts or green peas. If you did not ask for only a little your plate would be piled high. When I first entered college and did not know the form or when I was late in saying 'only a little please' I had the unfortunate experience of having my main dish smothered in vegetables. But Merton food was good and there was never anything I could not eat. After lunch I generally went to the graduates' common-room, the MCR.

Middle Common Room (MCR)

The MCR had been built in the thirteenth century as the warden's residence and remains much the same today. In particular, the fine old beams are still there. As I have explained above, the first time I was in the MCR was when I was introduced by the warden to J, the chairman, on my arrival at Merton. J had then introduced me in his room to other members of the MCR and invited me to drinks in the common-room. In a short time, after I had joined Merton, I had got to know most of the other members.

One of my main joys at Merton was to go up to the MCR after lunch, drink coffee and spend a short time there with the other members. The MCR was, of course, at its most lively immediately after lunch and dinner. However, after lunch most members could not dally very long and after some thirty minutes would say: 'I must get back to work.' Nevertheless, these moments with my fellow students, brief as they were, were very important for me. Coffee was freely available in the MCR and one or other of the members would pour it out into the cups provided. It was fairly strong coffee, but the conversation while we were drinking it was most enjoyable. It usually covered a wide variety of topics, but occasionally it focused on a single topic. I remember some of these. One topic, which led to a heated controversy, was whether as a result of the reduction in government contributions to university costs the decision not to award an honorary degree to Prime Minister Thatcher was right. Some students thought that the university's decision was natural in the circumstances while others argued that in view of her achievements and as she had graduated from the university she deserved the award. I refrained from taking sides and listened to the arguments which became heated; inevitably, the debate ended without any conclusion being reached. Another subject of discussion was the rights and wrongs of the introduction at Wimbledon of the system adopted at that time of judging by sound whether a service was in or out. One student laughingly suggested: 'With such thick glasses as are worn by the umpire it is surely very difficult to determine whether a service is in or out when the ball is travelling at such speed.' But another argued forcefully that Wimbledon did not need such a 'sound' system.

There was a notebook at the bar close to the door to the MCR; in this the server of coffee or someone else noted down the names of those who took coffee and the amounts owing were collected later. The same system applied to drinks from the MCRs minibar. At first I was unaware of this system and only after some time did I realize that I had been taking coffee and drinking liqueurs without paying up. I now realize and regret my error. I was surprised that the coffee cups, which were washed in lots of washing-up liquid, were not rinsed properly, but I gathered this was always the case in England. I do not know whether this is true or not.

Occasionally, when I went to the MCR, there would be nobody there. I would then glance through copies of *The Times*, *The Economist* and *Newsweek* which were laid out in the common room and I might spend some time looking at the leaflets announcing events in Oxford. Sometimes, I would lounge in a dilapidated armchair and just contemplate the white ceiling with its fine beams.

Each term there was an MCR dinner to which guests could be invited. Men would wear dinner jackets if they had them and ladies would come in evening dresses and other finery. The dinners were usually held in the Savile Room next to the dining hall while aperitifs would be served in the MCR. After a brief chat the party would move to the Savile Room. Port would be served at table and after the toast to the Queen was announced all joined in the toast saying 'The Queen!'. After coffee the party returned to the MCR where the conversation continued. I liked the general 'at home' atmosphere of these dinner parties and usually went to the dinners each term while I was at Oxford. In addition to members of the MCR various post-graduate students from outside the college attended these dinners and as a result I got to know a number of very interesting individuals.

I learnt about events sponsored by the MCR from printed notices or more often from colleagues after lunch. There were various events apart from the dinners such as theatre performances and excursions on the river.

After coffee in the MCR I often had more studying to do. Of course, on some days I had work to do until dinner time. In the intervals when I felt the need for exercise I would play tennis and go jogging to work up a sweat. I would also go into town to buy books and everyday articles.

Shopping and the English character

I would now like to write briefly about my shopping expeditions. In addition to notebooks, index cards and card cases required for my studies, and with help from my police escort, I also bought such daily necessities as drinks and fruit. When I had invited anyone to join me at the guest table I would buy wine and sherry at a shop nearby. Readers may perhaps have heard of William Morris (1877–1963), the founder of Morris Motors, later British Leyland (not to be confused with the famous artist also called William Morris.) Before he began to make motor cars he had worked in a bicycle shop. His bicycle shop had become the shop where I bought wine. (I wonder what has happened to it since.) I also went frequently to the newsagent's where they stocked lots of different magazines. They had a large variety of magazines relating to leisure pursuits and I often bought issues with information about canal tours which were relevant to my studies.

My regular paper was delivered every morning to my letter box in college, but if there had been some major event or I felt that I wanted to read another point of view I would look at a different newspaper. When I first went to Merton I was not used to English money. When I was told by the shop assistant that my purchases came to so many pounds or pence, I did not always hear properly what was said and either had to ask again or handed over the wrong sum. Another problem was that until I got accustomed to British money I used too many notes and collected too many heavy coins. On one occasion they all fell out of my purse. I was rather flustered but my police escort and people around, without making the slightest fuss, joined in picking up the coins. I recognized that I had made a blunder but as a result of this incident I was also struck by the kindliness of English people and I went back to college feeling relieved.

I appreciated the way in which English people after passing through a door would wait and keep the door open for the person behind. I can hardly remember any occasion when a door was closed in my face. When I was shopping I also noted that British people were good at forming queues and keeping their positions in the queue. I often saw long queues before the college dining hall and at bus stops. When I thought I was joining the end of a queue I was sometimes told that was not the end of the queue and I would take more care in future. Sometimes in a shop someone would ask 'Is this the end of the queue?' and I realized that there were established ways of forming queues. When I dropped my coins from my purse I was in a hurry to make my payment as there was a queue behind me.

However, in England it is rare to be hustled by people behind one in a queue even if one is taking rather a long time to pay; so perhaps I did not have to feel rushed.

The following was another blunder I made. There is a large covered market on the High Street and Cornmarket. Before I knew much about Oxford I went into the market and had difficulty in finding the way out among the maze of stalls selling everything from clothes to food and trinkets. Meat and fish could also be bought here. I was surprised to see a pheasant outside a stall which sold game and realized that in England shooting game was a popular sport. In one corner there was a shop selling fresh coffee. When I went there first and ordered some ground coffee the man behind the counter asked me whether I wanted it 'fine' or 'medium'. I did not understand what he meant and did not know how to reply. I managed to get by on this occasion and thus added some more words to my English vocabulary. There was also a pet shop in the market where, over a number of days, I saw the same parrot in a cage. I felt sorry for the bird which had not found a buyer. It was interesting to see so many different types of pets.

I took lots of photographs while I was at Oxford. When I went to look up documents in the library and public record office I always had a camera in the bottom of my bag. I never knew when I would be able to take a good shot in the town. There were three camera shops which I used to visit where my face was known and I would either be asked: 'Working hard?' or 'Are you enjoying your time at Oxford?' When I took in films for developing, normally I would be asked my name and address. But in one shop where I had been many times in the past and where the assistants knew my name and address these would be written on the envelope in which the films were sent up for developing without my needing to say a word. There was one assistant, who reminded me of someone who used to work for us. One day shortly before I was due to leave Oxford I went as usual to this shop and a young assistant on duty said to me: 'This is Ms ——'s last day in the shop and we are all having tea upstairs, won't you join us?' This was so unexpected and sudden an invitation that I hesitated for a moment before replying. I guessed that the assistant might be referring to the older lady I have mentioned and as she had been so helpful I thought that this would be a very good opportunity of expressing my thanks and accordingly joined the party. As I had surmised correctly the tea was in her honour. Many other members of the staff were present and we all enjoyed a lively conversation all about photography.

I enjoyed visiting shops selling new books as well as second-hand bookshops. I often went to Blackwell's and to Parkers'. At one second-hand book store in the High Street, where I bought etchings of Oxford, I was surprised to see many *Ukiyo-e* (Japanese prints). I saw at the top of one print of an exotic place the word *'Miyako'* (meaning capital i.e. Kyoto, the old capital) and the proprietor whom I knew asked me if it was of Japan. One day, passing by chance by the shop, I saw in the window an old map showing the route of the Thames; first thing on the following morning I went to the shop and bought it. I still have the map by me now and often refer to it. One day, in the antiquarian book corner in Blackwell's I came across some books which I needed for my studies but which I did not think I would ever be able to find. I clapped my hand with joy and bought them there and then. I also enjoyed buying records, CDs and music.

This has nothing to do with shopping, but when I was at Oxford I had my first experience of going into a bank. The reason was that I had been out of England visiting various other countries and wanted to change the foreign currency which I had acquired into English pounds. This might be my first and last experience of being in a bank. I also used a credit card to buy in Oxford shops, but I do not suppose I shall have the chance to shop in this way in the future. I used a barber's shop in the town to get my hair cut. The first time they looked at me rather oddly and my hair was cut rather roughly, but when I went there a second time I was greeted in a very friendly fashion with a warm 'Good Morning, Sir' and my hair was carefully trimmed. My haircut this time lasted about twice as long as on the first occasion. The barber chatted to me saying 'I saw an interesting television programme about Japan' and asked 'Do you like Oxford?' After this I always went to the same barber's shop while I was at Oxford. Over in England the barbers do not wash your hair unless you specially request it and I used to go back to college and wash my hair in the bath.

Draughts and baths

I must record that I suffered a bit in my daily existence from the cold including while taking a bath. The draughts were one cause of discomfort. There was no central heating in my rooms and the only source of heating was an electric heater in my study. So when I went to Merton I bought another electric heater for my bedroom, but the draughts coming through the cracks round my bedroom window were very cold. When we parted Colonel Hall had given me an electric blanket and told me to use it at Oxford; it had much use! With Mrs Fuji's help I managed to stop up the cracks. Another of my memories of the cold was in the bathroom. There was usually one bath on each floor in the college. I was fortunate enough to have my own separate bathroom in an adjoining room to which I could get without being seen by others, but when I half-filled the bath tub with hot water, the tap would run cold and I never had enough hot water for a really good hot soak! As there was no shower over the bath, when I washed my hair, I had to make do by filling the bath only a third full and rinse my hair in the basin into which I poured the remaining hot water. From this experience I realized why English people are not accustomed to lingering in the bath. To be honest, I began to long for a Japanese bath. I had realized from visiting Chedworth Roman Villa with Professor Mathias that the Romans had liked hot baths. Did the custom of enjoying hot baths leave Britain with the Romans? Be that as it may, I must say that now I feel a certain nostalgia for both the baths and the draughts. How to cope with them was one of the things I learned at Oxford.

Dinner

There were two sessions at dinner in Merton, perhaps because of the size of the hall. An informal dinner was served from 6.30 and a formal dinner from 7.30 and students could choose which one they wanted to go to. At the first session those attending could wear what they liked and it was a self-service meal. At the formal dinner you had to wear a gown and a tie. Any student who was incorrectly dressed or arrived late had to pay a forfeit and swallow a beer at one go. At the formal dinner the fellows sat at a high table on a dais at one end of the hall. When a mallet was struck on the table a representative of the students would come forward and recite a grace in Latin. In the British film *Chariots of Fire* one scene shows a college hall. Although this was at Cambridge, the scene at Merton was much the same. At dinner (informal or formal) the menu was the same, namely soup, meat and desert; coffee was not included. At the informal dinner you received a plate and a dish at the entrance and went on to the counter where the food was dished out on to your plates. Gravy and cooked vegetables were placed separately on the tables and you helped yourself as they were passed round. I particularly liked the almost over-cooked sprouts and I always took a large portion. Once an English friend sitting beside me asked how I could like such stuff so much! At the formal dinner you were served by the dining-room staff. Students were permitted to bring their own drinks into hall. Most either drank water or beer which was served to them at the door. There were stands just inside the door for coats and jackets which I sometimes used. Occasionally I forgot that I had left a garment there and would not collect it for some days, but it was generally where I had left it. It was very rare for any item to be stolen.

Twice a week guests could be invited if places had been reserved at the guest table. On these occasions students could bring in wine and enjoy leisurely chats with their guests. Apart from the enjoyment of looking down from the lobby onto the diners below the guests were able to enjoy specially prepared gourmet dishes. I asked Ambassador Hirahara and others from the Embassy to dine as my guests; they seemed pleased with the setting and the cuisine.

I should like to mention another aspect of dinner in hall. Every year there was a 'Brown Rice Week' which lasted a whole week. In order that a contribution could be made to the relief of famine in Africa and for assistance to refugees, at the formal dinner during this week only brown rice was served. Students taking dinner paid the same amount for their food as at other times and the difference between the costs of the normal menu and of brown rice was given to charity. I thought this an excellent scheme as it increased the understanding of students for those who were suffering. In the Michaelmas Term in 1983 £321 (the pound at that time was worth

348 yen) was contributed to the 'Save the Children Fund'. I went a number of times during 'Brown Rice Week' to formal dinners and found that brown rice alone left me feeling rather hungry, but I had the satisfaction of having performed a good deed. According to one student, the day on which I only had brown rice, the rice was the worst that week.

According to my records, while at Merton, the cost of breakfast was 43 pence, lunch 78 pence and dinner one pound. A student who took all meals in college naturally saved on his expenses. At Oxford, students were encouraged to take their meals in hall, but some wanting to save only took breakfast and dinner in college. Meals in colleges were not all equally good. Fortunately, while I was at Merton the college was reputed to have the best food in Oxford. This reputation dated back to the time when one undergraduate, deploring the poor quality of the food, contributed funds for the employment of a good chef. According to student gossip, a certain college had the worst food humans could eat.

Meals in college provided the best opportunity to get to know other students. Soon after I joined the college I noted that students sitting next to one another at table would introduce themselves and shake hands. I got to know many other students at meals in college. As I explain later it was through meeting someone at breakfast that I was able to form a string quartet. There were no fixed places for seating at meals. So I met many other students whose lively conversation ranged over a wide range of topics. These included, of course, the world scene, politics, economics, theatre, music, sports and other topics. I was asked about Japan and my researches and this led me to learn about many things which I had not known about before. When I went to Merton and was spoken to for the first time by a number of people one after the other I had a hard time, but as I began to make friends conversation became much easier. Meal times became an important element in my life. When students, who are studying a variety of different subjects, are living and taking meals together, they meet other students outside their own field with wide knowledge of other subjects. Conversations with them are an invaluable opportunity to widen one's own knowledge. This may be the reason why the university encouraged students to take meals in hall. Before

I left for Oxford my mother urged me to take meals in hall as often as possible, and to buy a good umbrella. I realize now what wise advice it was, and I am tremendously grateful.

Most students got through their meals quickly and speedily emptied their plates conversing all the while. I would often find that I was the only one who still had a full plate! I was struck by the fact that other students could eat so quickly while talking. The way in which students conversed with all and sundry around them was quite different from what happens in Japanese universities.

High table

While I was at Oxford I was fortunate in having many opportunities of taking meals at high table both at Merton and at other colleges.

I should like to explain more about high table and will base my remarks on my experience of high table at Merton. Sherry is served as an aperitif in the senior common room. Then, after some conversation, the group moves downstairs to the high table in the dining hall for the meal. I have already related how the dinner begins. The first time I sat down at high table at Merton I was astonished by the array of silver. I did not examine each piece, but at one college I noticed a piece of silver with a hallmark for 1624. When I first dined at high table at Merton I did not know most of the staff at the table other than Dr Highfield. Sitting opposite me was someone who looked a typical Oxford don; he said to me abruptly: 'Japanese drive on the left as we do in Britain, don't they?' I promptly replied: 'yes, that's the case' and then he turned to the don sitting next to him and said: 'but until quite recently there was one part of Japan where they drove on the right; that was on the island of Okinawa'. To be frank, I was astonished. I had expected that at Merton the conversation might turn to Japan, but I did not think the subject would be broached in quite that way.

The next thing that surprised me was that the food at high table was so much better than that served to the students. Unfortunately, I do not have by me the menu for that day, but I do remember that we began with smoked salmon and we had a full-course dinner including dessert. For students it was an honour to be invited to dine at high table, but it was a bit of an ordeal to eat with the dons. Later, one student said to me: 'Everyone seems to have problems talking with the dons at high table. The trouble is that the dons know too much.' I nodded, but in fact I always enjoyed being invited to join the dons at high table and I managed to get by in conversation with them.

I will now say a few words about occasions when I was invited to the high table in other colleges. Professor Ugawa Kaoru of Rikkyo University once arranged for me to be invited to the high table in Somerville as the guest of Dr Harvey, a scholar of medieval history. I asked her many questions about her special field of study and her replies were, of course, valuable for my research. But I remember noticing that there were many men among the students. Somerville, which only took women students, was Prime Minister Thatcher's college. So I asked the principal of the college by whose side I was sitting: 'Since when has the college admitted male students?' She promptly replied: 'The reason why there are so many men here tonight is that this is a guest evening and the students have brought along their boyfriends.' What a silly question to have asked her, I thought, and still blush at the memory.

I was also privileged to be invited to the high tables at colleges such as Exeter, Brasenose, Worcester, Magdalen and New College.

Magdalen College (which, curiously, is pronounced 'Maud-lin') has a very odd custom for their high-table guests. I was introduced to Magdalen by a musical friend who had connections with the college and was invited by the master to join the high table. As at other colleges aperitifs were served in a separate room but the way we went to the dining hall was different. We all went along the roof of the cloisters and I remember that the guests who had been invited for the first time, having signed their name in the guest book, were then asked to weigh themselves on an old weighing machine in the form of a chair. The weights were calculated in stones (one stone equals 6.4 kilograms) as is the custom in Britain.

Invitations I received were issued by the authorities of the colleges where I had got to know the dons or the master or in the case of Somerville through the intervention of a friend. At St John's I was invited by a student, whom I had come across and who was studying Japanese, to join the students' table. At one seminar at the

Nissan Institute of Japanese Studies, which had been established at St Antony's as a result of a gift from the company, I got to know one of the fellows of St John's and was invited as a guest to dinner in the senior common room. St John's was, apart from Merton, the only college at Oxford where I dined at both the students' table and the fellows'. I thought that the food was rather better at Merton, but it was not bad at St John's.

I enjoyed dining with fellows at all the colleges and it was interesting to observe the students. There were colleges where it was not necessary to wear gowns. While in some colleges, the hall was so small that students had to sit squashed together on forms close to the walls. When someone had finished eating and wanted to leave, it was impossible to get out unless one climbed up onto the table and walked along it, which some students did, in their shoes! At another college, where so few people attended meals I asked why, and was told that students kept away because the food was so poor. It may not seem to matter greatly whether the food was good or not, but the fact that the food at Merton was good attracted students to eat in hall, thus encouraging them to get to know one another and learn a lot from one another. There are various arguments about English food. One friend of mine said: 'The English don't pay much attention to food. They prefer to concentrate on improving their houses and put their energies, for example, into painting their house. In France the opposite applies. They concentrate on the food and don't bother about their house.' What do readers think? Is this assertion fair?

After-dinner drinks and fruit are served in a separate room. Port is usually the first choice, but Madeira (a red desert wine from the island of Madeira, a Portuguese possession) and a sweet white wine (usually Sauterne from the Bordeaux area) are also available. The way in which port is served is interesting. Each person pours the port into his own glass and passes the port on to his neighbour. The port must be circulated in the clock-wise direction. When I first took port I apparently made a mistake in passing the wine; seeing the looks of horror on the faces of the dons I realized that I must have passed the wine in the wrong direction. When I enquired whether this was the case, most of the dons said 'That is the custom in England'. On the other hand, one Merton fellow who specialized in law gave a different reply: 'It is done to fool the witches.' I thought this explanation made sense because during the Middle Ages witches were regarded as abnormal beings. Dr Highfield explained to me that, when a table plan is prepared, the host (usually the warden or the master) has the chief guest on his right and the port is passed from the chief guest to the host and so on clockwise. English people are mostly right-handed and the port glass is thus placed in front of the guest on the right side. Port is normally served in a fairly heavy decanter and it is easier to take hold of the decanter with the right hand. I learnt that the reason why English people like port so much is because at the time of negotiations between Methuen, the British Envoy to Portugal, and the Portuguese government at the beginning of the eighteenth century it was agreed that the tariff on port should be decreased thus favouring port as against French wines. I need hardly add that the name port comes from Oporto, the harbour from which port was exported from Portugal.

There were various ways in which I passed the time after dinner. When I was under pressure to prepare for tutorials or absorbed in my research I would generally spend the time in my room. On other occasions I might visit friends in their flats or have visitors in my rooms or I might go to concerts or pass the time in the MCR. In the past it was a special feature of Oxford that if you stayed out late and missed the curfew when the college gate was shut you had to climb over the college wall when you came home. Merton's gate was closed at midnight in term time and at 11 o'clock in the vacations, but students could get a key to the wooden gate at the back of the college and anyone who was late and had a key could get back into college without climbing the wall. Similar arrangements must have been made in other colleges.

Weekends

At weekends I played tennis or music or visited the houses of friends, but I also enjoyed myself very much by taking photographs in Oxford and driving around the neighbouring countryside. I shall write about these drives later. One of my biggest tasks at weekends was doing my washing. Fortunately, there were three washing machines and a drier, with a drying room attached, in the basement of the building in St Alban's quad. When I joined Merton I was told how to use these machines and when the weekend came round I used them. All I had to do was put my washing in the machine, pour in the appropriate quantity of detergent and insert the money, but as I was not used to the procedure it was a bit of puzzle for me. The first time I used the machines I made a major mistake. As instructed I put in my washing, the detergent and the money. I gathered that the washing would be ready in forty minutes; so I went back to the basement forty minutes later, only to find that there were soap suds all around. When I looked carefully I discovered that soap suds had clearly come from the machine I had been using. There was another student looking fed up near the machine who asked: 'Is this yours? The soapsuds have over-flown.' I had overloaded the machine with washing. I apologized to him and did my best to get over the difficulties I had caused. I still have a good laugh at my mishap. The other student turned out to be a German called H who was a member of the MCR whom I got to know as a result of this incident.

When the washing was finished all I had to do was to put it in the drier. It was a delicate matter to get the timing right. If a lot of students were using the machines and you were a bit late in collecting your washing you might find it displayed on top of the machine. This was because when a student wanting to use the machine found that the previous man's washing had dried, he would take it out and replace it with his own. This happened to me on several occasions, but I never lost anything as a result. After they had been dried, shirts had to be ironed. Immediately after I began at Oxford I went into the city and bought an iron and an iron-stand. I learnt how to use the iron from one of my police escorts. I did not find it too difficult to learn and while I was studying at Oxford I did all my own ironing. This was one of my Oxford experiences.

I have already often mentioned my police escorts: I must say a little more about them. During my two years at Oxford I was provided with two police officers from the Metropolitan Police who were responsible for my safety. One was called Roger Bacon; it is rather difficult to describe him, but he was very much an Englishman. The other was called Bruce Ayer, a charming man, who spoke

English with a Scottish accent that was easy to understand. They were opposite in character but both good men. They took it in weekly turns to occupy the room next to mine and to provide round the clock protection. As far as I was concerned they did more than provide protection. They were excellent guides to English life. They made all sorts of arrangements for me and helped me with my understanding of documents which were difficult to read. I also got them to read letters for me and they did all sorts of administrative tasks as well. Whenever I went out one of them would always go with me, but they were never obtrusive. Roger Bacon's name will lead some readers to recall that of the famous English philosopher Roger Bacon (1214–94) who lived in the neighbourhood of Folly Bridge in Oxford and carried out astronomical observations from a building there which at a later time was rebuilt at vast expense. It is said that people called a building which looked absurd a 'folly' and that is why the bridge is called 'Folly Bridge'. There is also a narrow street in Oxford called 'Roger Bacon Lane'. When Roger, my police offer, came across it he was delighted. The favourite phrase of Bruce, the other officer, was 'Oh dear!' When anything happened these were the first words he uttered. During the two years they were with me I never had any unpleasant moments. They provided me with every possible help during this time and I shall never forget all they did for me.

Family visits

During my time at Oxford visits from my family gave me a great deal of pleasure. In the second half of February 1984 my parents made a tour of Africa and stopped off in Belgium. His Majesty the King of the Belgians very kindly invited me to come over to Brussels so that I could meet my parents, whom I had not seen for some time, and we were able to have an enjoyable time together. The King and Queen and my parents had had a long-standing friendship and I greatly appreciated this unexpected opportunity to meet them again. My parents were also able to pay a short visit to London on their way back from Africa that April and I was able to give them a tour of Oxford. On the way to Oxford we called at Colonel Hall's home where we all had tea with him and his family and my parents were able to see where

I had lived for three months. I had told them in my letters about my life there, but there is a real difference between what you can learn from letters and what you see for yourself. They were shown around Merton by Sir Rex Richards and Dr Highfield and they were able to meet some of my close friends. Sir Rex gave a lunch for them in the senior common room and invited Professor Mathias, Dr Highfield and several Merton students to join us for lunch. For lunch that day the Merton College chef, whose face I recognized, grilled the meat near the door of the common room. The meal was one of the best meals I had at Merton. I was very pleased by the care and consideration for my parents, who had come from so far away, shown by Sir Rex, the college chef and others at Oxford who were present.

In the afternoon I showed them round Oxford. We went first to St Mary's Church, from whose tower we had a good view over the city of Oxford, and I pointed out the main sites. I also took them to University and New Colleges. My father had visited Oxford in 1953 when at the age of nineteen he had attended the coronation of Queen Elizabeth and had stayed with the master of University College. On that occasion he had planted a cherry tree; he was delighted to find that it had grown into a big tree in the thirty-one years since he had been in Oxford. The room in which my father had slept had changed a good deal in the interim but I shall not forget the nostalgic look on my father's face when he saw it once again. From University College we crossed the High Street and went on to All Souls where I had my tutorials. Guided by Professor Mathias we went into his room where he sat on a sofa, asking me to sit beside him, thus re-enacting one of my tutorials.

From Oxford we went on to visit Broughton Castle where Lord and Lady Saye and Sele and their son William received us warmly. It was a most enjoyable family gathering and we were all able to relax together. I had discussed with the ambassador and members of the staff of the Japanese Embassy in London plans for them to visit Oxford and Broughton Castle. So it was rewarding to see that my parents could relax after their long, tiring and anxious journey. That evening we were able to enjoy some music and played a trio. Lady Saye and I both played the viola while my mother played the piano. It was a long time since we had played together.

In July of that same year my younger sister Princess Sayako [Nori no Miya] visited Oxford after a few days 'home stay' with Colonel and Mrs Hall. I showed her round Merton and Oxford and accompanied her to the pretty village of Broadway some forty kilometres north-west of Oxford, where we enjoyed a fine view of the countryside from a nearby hill. She liked best the views of Christ Church Meadow and of the country near Broadway. In March 1985 my younger brother Prince Akishino visited Oxford. I took him up the chapel tower at Merton and to Christ Church Meadow. From the top of the chapel tower Dr Highfield pointed out to him the main buildings in Oxford. In the evening, I took my brother to a Chinese restaurant which I had been to a number of times before. He was able to converse with the restaurant staff in Chinese, a language which he had studied at university. He later also became a student at Oxford and I hope that his visit proved useful in that connection. Thus, in my two years at Oxford all my close family visited me. It was a real joy to be able to show them around.

With Oxford students

1. VISITING STUDENTS' FLATS AND GOING OUT

At Merton the best time to enjoy talking with one's friends was in the evenings after dinner. I should now like to write briefly about the friends I made chiefly at Oxford.

Shortly after I went up to Merton I got to know a very pleasant couple. The man had come up to Oxford at the same time as I had and was reading English Literature at Merton. The girl was doing research at a different university but they were always together and no one doubted that she was also at Merton. P and his fiancée were very kind to me while I was at Oxford and they greatly helped to make my stay at Oxford so enjoyable. I got to know P at the first MCR dinner after term began. Thereafter they often came to my rooms for a chat. P was learning to play the *shakuhachi* (a Japanese five-holed bamboo wind instrument) and his fiancée was interested in Japanese design. They both showed great interest in Japan. One day, they asked me what was the word for 'lazy' in Japanese. I told them that the appropriate translation was '*namakemono*'. P immediately memorized the word and pointing to his fiancée called her '*namakemono*'. They still use some Japanese words when they write to me these days. They also asked me what was the Japanese for 'Your Highness'. I explained that the word was '*denka*' and said that this should not be confused with the electric light in the ceiling to which I pointed and which was called '*denki*' in Japanese. Afterwards, I regretted saying this but it was too late and thereafter the two of them teased me by referring to me as '*denki*' and pointing at the light said that it was '*denka*'. One day P came round with his *shakuhachi* and persuaded me to blow into it, but I could not get a peep out of it. He then produced some good sounds from the instrument and declared in his typical way, as he blew into the instrument, 'I am Samurai!'

They were not the only ones whom I entertained in my rooms. Another was J, the girl who had walked beside me when we went to the matriculation ceremony at the beginning of the first term. She was studying Japanese and had visited Japan; we often spoke of the difficulties which Japanese had in learning English. I used to serve *senbei* (rice crackers) to students who visited me. I was interested to find why some liked *senbei* covered in seaweed and others did not. English people seem to have an antipathy to seaweed. When, later on, I visited Wales someone in a speech declared: 'We Welsh people eat seaweed in the same way as you do in Japan.' The implication was that Welsh people when eating seaweed were closer to Japanese than English people.

I often went to pubs with P and his fiancée. One pub which we frequented was the *Turf Tavern*, which I shall refer to later when discussing music at Oxford. They taught me the meaning of the term 'pub crawl'. I gathered that it involved going to at least ten pubs and drinking a pint of beer at each. True or false it was an interesting piece of information for me. On their recommendation I also tried various types of beer in a pub. I found that there were all sorts of bitter as well as many kinds of lager. Talking of pubs I found that there were a number of pubs on the banks of the Thames set in beautiful scenery. At a pub in the north of Oxford called *The Perch* (a perch is a type of fresh water fish) meals were served at tables with chairs in the garden. From there one could walk along a stretch of promenade by the river. It was a good place to spend the middle of the day in the summer. The *Trout Inn* was not far from there along the river bank. From the *Trout* you could hear the water flowing over a weir and see a Chinese-style wooden bridge; this gave an exotic flavour to the scene of the pub and the river. Accompanied by my police escort I once cycled from Merton and visited all three pubs in the area, *The Perch*, *The Trout* and *The White Hart*.

I also went with my friends to restaurants as well as to pubs. There were no Japanese restaurants in Oxford, but there were Chinese, Indian, Italian and French restaurants as well as others serving the food of the countries from which the proprietors came. I generally found the food at Merton appetising and did not often long for Japanese cuisine. But Chinese food and curry did not cost much and made me think of Japan. We also often went to pizza and spaghetti places as well as to fish-and-chip shops where we bought cod, herring, plaice or some other white fish with chips doused in vinegar and wrapped in newspaper. As fish and chips at the time of the industrial revolution were an important source of protein for workers, this was one of the tastes which I found relevant to the period of my studies.

I was also invited by members of the MCR to go to wine bars which served cocktails. We did not know one cocktail from another; so we each ordered different ones and, though this was rather bad behaviour, sampled by drinking through straws those ordered by others. I also went to a disco in the city to see what it was like. Here I made a real blunder. I remember that it occurred on a Saturday evening. I went with another man who was a member of the MCR and who apparently liked discos. We were stopped at the door and when I asked why I was told that on that evening people in T shirts and jeans were not admitted. As usual I was in jeans and my companion was wearing a T shirt. The door-keeper pointed to my police escort who was behind us and said 'You will do!' He was not wearing a tie but he was wearing a blazer and thus apparently qualified. While I was at Oxford I tried as far as possible to be like other students and certainly did not explain who I was. So I gave up and went weakly away. I learnt through this experience some new information, namely that at discos in Oxford at the weekend a certain standard of dress was required.

While I was at Oxford I generally wore informal clothes such as jeans when I went out. When Japanese tourists saw me thus garbed they looked as though they could hardly believe their eyes. When some young Japanese girls saw me in jeans one day they spluttered 'It's a lie' (i.e. I can't believe it!). Not knowing what they meant by 'a lie' I did not know how to respond. My first attempt to visit a disco having ended in failure I went on the next occasion in a mixed group of men and girls from the MCR to a different disco. As this was my first time in a disco I felt overwhelmed by the noise in the hall. On the dance floor I saw young people dancing all sorts of steps. So I joined them doing my own kind of dance steps and finding myself face to face with a girl from the MCR. I was not in the least bored. It was two o'clock in the morning before we left. Perhaps this was the first and the last disco I would go to in my life.

I should like to add a few words about visits to friends' flats. One day, I went to C's flat, the MCR treasurer who was a vegetarian. C and a friend made a vegetarian dish for us. I recall that it was a bit unique although not much to my taste, but we had an interesting conversation. C was very keen on films, so much so that he made his own films. We had a really varied discussion and of course we talked that evening about films we had enjoyed. Those who lived outside college generally had flats with kitchens so that they could cook their own meals. In my second year I was invited to a wine-and-cheese party by M, the American who was chairman of the MCR. His fiancée was a French woman and I was surprised by how many different sorts of cheeses there were at the party that evening. There were quite a few members of the MCR present and I learnt a lot from them about cheese and wine.

M was also very fond of films. M and C arranged for videos they had chosen to be shown in the MCR after dinner. When I said that I had not seen many Hitchcock films they immediately borrowed some. I thought *Psycho*, *The Birds* and *Rear Window* were particularly good films. When members of the MCR sat round and watched Visconti's film *Death in Venice* on television it was so exciting that I had difficulty in getting to sleep that night. M or C kindly let me know when there was something worth watching and C always brought me a glass of Chartreuse while I was watching the programme. Only afterwards did I realize that he had treated me to these drinks.

I visited a number of other flats. I was invited to the home of a foreign student from Oman to a meal where his state's cuisine was served. I was also asked to lunch by a student from Singapore who was a member of another college and we had a good meal which resembled Japanese '*shabu-shabu*'. On another occasion I was invited to his house by K, an American student, to join him for a meal. We were joined by K's brothers and cousins who were also studying at Oxford. We had a noisy evening and ended up with an enjoyable concert on the banjo. K's elder brother R was teaching at New College and invited me to the high table there. R was later appointed to the staff of Princeton while I was at Oxford. In 1985 at the end of my time at Oxford I went home via America and was able to stay a night at his home in West Virginia. When I visited Princeton where he was then teaching he arranged for me to be introduced to Brook Shields the American film star.

2. VARIOUS GROUP ACTIVITIES AT OXFORD

There are all kinds of groups at Oxford. The groups with which I was directly involved were the Oxford Japan Society (OJS), the karate and judo groups and the dramatic society. I was either honorary president or an honorary member of these groups. The OJS was made up of students studying Japanese and of Japanese students at Oxford. The Society contributed to the understanding of Japan by organizing lectures on Japanese culture and society, putting on Japanese films, arranging tea ceremony demonstrations and showing how to prepare and cook Japanese food. Each term the OJS circulated a printed programme of their activities and whenever I could I went along to any of their meetings which I thought would be interesting. I was able to see famous productions directed by Ozu Yasujiro and Mizoguchi Kenji and to have my fill of Japanese films while I was in England. Of course, Japanese films were shown with English subtitles. At OJS demonstrations Japanese dishes and beer could be sampled and these were particularly popular occasions. I also attended Japanese dinners and *koto*[1] performances. As a result, I got to know many students who were deeply interested in Japan as well as many Japanese students at the university.

---

[1] A *koto* is a form of Japanese zither used from early times.

I should add a few remarks about a Japanese language lecture which I observed. There was a conversation class that day, in the course of which there was a discussion in Japanese about how to learn Japanese and the advantages and disadvantages of various methods. The main theme was about the role of Chinese characters (*kanji*) in the Japanese language. Would it be a good idea to do away with Chinese characters? Some suggested that this would greatly reduce the problem of reading Japanese and increase the amount of time available for the study of other languages. I was asked to comment. As far as I remember, I pointed out that Chinese characters were ideograms and thus made it possible to absorb sentences quickly. Moreover, there were many words in Japanese with the same sounds but different meanings and *kanji* made it possible to distinguish between words with the same sounds. For instance, if you say '*kami wo kiru*' where '*kiru*' means 'to cut', '*kami*' can mean both 'paper' and 'hair'. One of the students at this class is engaged these days in research into Japanese art. He was an undergraduate at St John's and invited me to dinner in his college. I was glad to note that all those who were studying Japanese were good students. I expect that they will all be playing major parts in Anglo-Japanese relations.

My connection with the karate club came about because one of the members of the MCR belonged to the club. He invited me to watch a practice. I never learnt how to do karate, but I was interested to learn what induced Oxford students to take it up and how karate was practised at the club. A Japanese karate expert who was teaching in the USA happened to be in Oxford at that time and was coaching members of the club. I was, therefore, able to observe carefully how karate was practised at the club. Shortly after this I was asked to become an honorary member of the club and on some occasions I went along to the club to watch training sessions. I noted that Japanese terms were invariably used and that it came naturally to the students to refer to the teacher as '*Sensei*'. On one occasion after the session I had a leisurely chat and a beer with members of the club. I was impressed by the fact that many of the members, who included a number of women, had taken up karate with the aim of building up their strength of mind. As I was only made an honorary member of the judo club shortly before I left Oxford I did not have a chance to see them training. However, I asked a number of members of the club to tea in my rooms and we were able to have a chat. As a result of this meeting I was able last year to meet a number of Oxford judo players while they were in Tokyo. I shall comment on the Oxford dramatic society later.

3. CONTACTS WITH OXFORD UNDERGRADUATES AND DONS

Oxford University students generally work hard. This is due to a large extent to the tutorial system, but it is also relevant that each term undergraduates have to take examinations, popularly called 'collections', and undergo regular tests of their academic abilities. Students express their own opinions clearly in various debates and seminars and in their everyday conversations. The dons expect students to express their own opinions in the essays which they present at tutorials. I was surprised by the wide education of Oxford students. Whenever they got together they never had any difficulty in starting up a conversation, finding a subject in which all present were interested and pursuing the topic. In a word, they were experts in social intercourse. They were never reserved and shy at parties. To celebrate my birthday I gave a party at Merton and invited a large number of fellow students to it. As host I did not have to worry about how the party would go; the guests made it go with a swing. My only concern was that my guests who were not used to drinking Japanese saké might enjoy it too much. As I feared, a number suffered from a bad hangover.

The interest of Oxford students in Japan was primarily in Japanese science and technology and the Japanese economy. With some exceptions they did not seem to know much about Japanese culture. Thus, they knew what such and such a company produced and its special characteristics, but some did not know whether Japan lay to the north or the south of the equator. Even so, however, I was pleased to find that a lot of them knew about origami and bonsai.

Another characteristic of Oxford students was that they dressed simply and frugally, but you could not miss the fact that there was a wide variety in what they wore. They were quite content to appear in torn jeans and sweaters with darns but it was interesting to observe how their individual preferences were shown in the mixture of colours in what they wore. In the evening I saw many students going to parties wearing dinner jackets. The women who wore drab or sober colours during the day would appear in all their finery in the evenings as there seemed to be many spots in Oxford where this was expected. It seemed to me that possibly the confidence gained from knowing how to dress to perfection must have made their ordinary clothes seem unimportant to them.

Most students at Oxford had their own bicycles. There are many one-way streets in Oxford and parking is not permitted in most streets in the city centre. This made it inconvenient to go around by car and one saw lots of students cycling to and from the library or research facilities. On the first day on which I rode a bicycle in Oxford, one student called out to me: 'I see that you have now become a real Oxford student.' I realized that students and bicycles were inseparable at Oxford. All student cycles were so old that it seemed as if the wheels might fall off while they were being ridden. Only a few students had cars. When you lived in college it was much more convenient to use a bicycle. For those living outside the same did not apply. I was occasionally given lifts by a graduate student whose car, too, was old and you never knew when it might break down. When it came to both clothes and vehicles, it seemed to be the fashion for Oxford students to go on using them in spite of their being old and somewhat dirty.

Readers may conclude from all the above that all Oxford students were outstanding students, but there were a number of odd people at Oxford. I have already mentioned the girl with a star mark on her forehead; there were also some students who dressed in punk style. Some were too clever and their statements sometimes outrageous. Talking of bright people, in the year when I went to Merton a girl at the tender age of thirteen was admitted to read mathematics. She did better than any other maths student and although no one can graduate unless they have completed three years at the university she took the final exam at the end of her second year.

There were also some odd people among the dons who might best be described as eccentrics. One went out in midwinter wearing nothing over his shirt, another never had his hair cut, yet another did all his research in a room with the curtains drawn. Generally speaking, however, dons were so knowledgeable that they were virtually walking dictionaries. I have already mentioned that some under-graduates when invited to a meal at high table found it difficult keeping up with the conversation as the dons were too sharp and knew too much. I heard of one don at Merton who at a quiz was the only person who answered all the questions correctly.

Lewis Carroll, the well known author of *Alice in Wonderland*, whose real name was Dodgson, was a don at Oxford. His college was Christ Church where he taught mathematics. Liddell, the master of Christ Church, had three daughters. Going up the river by boat one day with them and a colleague and being asked to tell a story he recounted a story which had Alice, the second daughter, as its main character. This became *Alice in Wonderland*. T. E. Lawrence, the main character in the film *Lawrence of Arabia*, was a fellow of All Souls.

I have written in these chapters about students and dons at Oxford, but I would like to record here how fortunate I was while I was at Oxford to have the help of Sir Rex Richards, the warden, Professor Mathias and Dr Highfield. I shall write about Professor Mathias and Dr Highfield in a later chapter, but I cannot find ade-quate words to express here my deep appreciation of the kindness of Sir Rex Richards. I had one year with him as warden. He invited me to tea and to meals in his house with other students and always kept an eye on my life as a student in his college. Shortly before I left Merton the new warden Dr Roberts assumed his post, but Sir Rex had been warden during the most important part of my stay and looked after me so well.

I have recently had the chance to read Adam Smith's *The Wealth of Nations*. He won a scholarship to study at Oxford and spent seven years at Balliol from 1740. In a dire critique of the situation then pre-vailing at Oxford he wrote: 'In the university of Oxford, the greater part of the public professors have, for these many years, given up altogether even the pretence of teaching.'[2] Now, two-hundred-and-fifty years later, so far as I could see, there was not the slightest sign that Oxford was anything like what Adam Smith had described. It seemed to me to be an educational establishment which was out-standing both in terms of scholarship and teaching.

---

[2] Book Five, Chapter 1, Part 3 of *The Wealth of Nations*

CHAPTER 6

CULTURAL LIFE AT OXFORD

———————□———————

Films, theatre and music

All sorts of events took place in Oxford. In addition to films and concerts there were performances of plays, musicals etc. There were Phoenix cinemas as well as ABC theatres in the town. I quite often went to the cinema, partly to improve my English, when good films or ones which had had good reviews or were interesting were shown in Oxford. I have already mentioned the film about Gandhi. I enjoyed the 007 series of *Octopussy* films and was interested to see David Lean's *Passage to India*. I thought the latter very well directed and I shall never forget the fine performance of Peggy Ashcroft as the leading lady in the film. Once, a friend of mine from a certain country, who was a student at Merton, invited some of us to see a film produced in his country which he, himself, had not yet seen. But it turned out to be pretty incomprehensible and he kept on apologizing for inflicting the film on us, although you can never really tell whether a film is good or bad unless you see it for yourself.

I went a number of times to the Oxford Playhouse which was run by the Oxford University Dramatic Society (OUDS). The OUDS, incidentally, elected me as Honorary President. On one occasion after the performance I went to the reception attended by former members of the OUDS. There were many famous people there, but unfortunately I did not know who was who and could not put names to faces. I learnt at this time that Peggy Ashcroft, John Gielgud, Richard Burton, Peter Brook and other famous stage people had close connections with Oxford, even if they were not necessarily members of the OUDS. After I had returned home in 1988 OUDS came to Japan to give some performances: on that occasion I was able to enjoy a performance of Shakespeare's *As you like it* at the Globe theatre in Shibuya. It was a very good performance and made me feel nostalgic about my time at Oxford.

I have already mentioned that when I was staying at Colonel and Mrs Hall's I had been to Stratford-on-Avon and seen *Henry VIII*. After joining Merton I was invited to join a group of members of the MCR to visit the Royal Shakespeare Theatre at Stratford to see *Twelfth Night, The Comedy of Errors* and other plays. The texts are all difficult to understand; so I used to read the story before going to see the play and so managed to follow the plot. I was surprised to see *The Comedy of Errors* produced in such a modern fashion. One of the characters was a policeman, in a contemporary uniform and riding on a bicycle. One of my companions muttered to me after the performance: 'Do you think Shakespeare would approve?'

Performing plays was a very popular pastime at Oxford. In the summer amateurs from the colleges would put on outdoor performances. At Merton these were done on a temporary stage in the back garden. Of course there was a charge for tickets, but alcohol was served in the interval and it made a good evening. In my first year I missed the performance as, for some reason or other, I had gone out that evening, but in my second year a *Commedia Dell'Arte* play was performed and I was urged by a Canadian friend, who was playing the part of a gate-keeper, to come along to the performance. So I went with a number of other fellow-students. Our friend suddenly appeared on the stage, said his two or three lines and hurriedly left the stage. It is quite a different experience when someone you know is performing. I thought that he had performed his part well, but one of those sitting near me thought it quite ordinary. I could have had a good view of the play from beginning to end without paying if I had used binoculars and looked out from the window of my room, but I would have missed the atmosphere. One evening, while performances were taking place in the garden and I was working in my room, I heard a roaring sound. I discovered it was pouring with rain. When I looked out into the garden to see what had happened to the play I saw that brilliant lights had been turned on and the play was continuing while the audience got drenched. Soon, as is common with English weather, the rain stopped, but I thought it must have been tough for the performers and the audience. I heard that Dr Highfield had been one of the victims of the shower.

I learnt that on another day there was to be an amateur production of *A Midsummer Night's Dream* in the garden at Magdalen. So I decided to go along. I was particularly struck by the fairies, who had put black paint all over themselves. This may be normal in Britain; I thought it an excellent idea for the fairies who wanted to remain invisible in the darkness.

I also went to concerts from time to time. The performers varied; in some concerts the performers were mainly Oxford students but in others British and foreign professionals performed. Concerts put on at Merton included performances by the Kodály Choir in the college chapel. I also went to an excellent performance of Haydn's *The Creation* in the Sheldonian Theatre by the choir of New College. This hall is the place where Haydn performed his 92nd Symphony, the one he selected from his many symphonies as an expression of his gratitude to the University for conferring on him in 1791 an honorary degree of doctor of music. As some of you may know, the 92nd is now called the *Oxford Symphony*. I was much moved by being able to hear a work by Haydn in this hall with its historical connections with him. I was also invited from time to time by a student of Queens with whom I played tennis to attend chamber music concerts at his college. The conductor was one of my music friends who taught music at Brasenose.

I also enjoyed opera. I was invited to Covent Garden Opera House in London by Prince Charles and Princess Diana to see Mussorgsky's *Boris Godunov*. I was also invited by the Royal Opera to see Rossini's *The Barber of Seville*. I remember vividly going twice to the opera at Glyndebourne. In my first year I saw Richard Strauss's *Arabella* and in the following year Rossini's *La Cenerentola*. Glyndebourne is an aristocratic country house some ninety kilometres south of London where operas and concerts are performed every year. Men wear dinner-jackets and women evening dress. In the interval members of the audience enjoy special Glyndebourne-style picnics in the garden.

I still remember clearly how much I enjoyed the opera as well as the excellent picnic and the conversation which accompanied it.

There was one other opera occasion while I was at Oxford which I will never forget. That was a performance in English by an English opera company at the Apollo Theatre of Wagner's *The Mastersingers of Nuremburg*. I was very interested to hear a Wagner opera performed in English. I wondered whether the beauty of the original would be lost in translation, but I need not have worried. In the interval I met by chance a member of the MCR and asked his opinion. His view was much the same as mine. I wanted to ask a German member of the MCR what he thought, but he was not there and so I was unable to seek his opinion. As it was such a long opera there were a number of intervals. During the long interval we remained in our seats and ate the sandwiches which we had brought with us. Many other members of the audience did the same. The performance began at 5.0 p.m. and ended at 10.50 p.m. Bruce, my police escort who had been sitting next to me, had looked downcast and had not been looking forward to the evening, but after it was over he muttered: 'Not too bad.'

Finally, in the context of concerts I should like to refer to the Holywell Music Room in Hollywell Street. This dates from 1740 and was the first purpose-built hall in Europe designed for musical performances. I went there on many occasions. It was here that I heard the Allegri Quartet and on one cold winter's evening at the beginning of November I heard an English singer give a rendering of Schubert's *Winterreise* which I found very moving. I was also invited to a *shakuhachi* recital by my friend P who, as I explained earlier, had taken up the instrument. The hall was intended for Western music but I thought that the *shakuhachi* sounded well there. The hall was near the *Turf Tavern*, a pub which I have mentioned previously. One of the precious memories of my time as a student at Oxford is of discussing music, while drinking beer, with my friends after concerts at Holywell Music Room.

I shall also never forget attending an international get-together of viola players in the Isle of Man. The Isle of Man is an island in the Irish Sea about half way between England and Ireland. It is known for Manx cats (cats without tails) and for the motor-bike races which

Oxford colleges along the High Street, looking from St Mary's Church towards Magdalen

2

General view of Oxford

3

Merton, Front Quad in the snow

4

Merton, middle common room

5

Merton, St Alban's Quad; my rooms were on the second floor of the building on the right

6

All Souls

The Thames near Oxford with Christ Church Meadow on the left

8

Christ Church Meadow

9

Lock on the upper reaches of the Thames near Lechlade

With Dr Highfield (centre)

With fellow students

are held there. I attended the International Viola Players Association on the island in August 1984. At the meetings I heard famous viola players give lessons and recitals and from talking with others at the meeting I learnt a good deal about playing the viola and composing music. The purpose of the congress was to enable famous viola players and those with connections with viola-playing from many countries to meet and to promote friendship among the participants as well as an understanding of the viola through recitals and lessons. Although the Isle of Man is part of the United Kingdom it has its own parliament and bank notes. As a result, while it is termed a crown dependency and has the Queen as its sovereign, it is largely an independent state. Motor-bike racing can be held in the Island because the English law forbidding such racing on English roads does not apply in the Isle of Man. The island's banknotes cannot be torn as they are printed on material containing plastic. You also find locally-issued banknotes in Scotland and in the Channel Islands.

Enjoying chamber music

I was particularly glad to be able to take part in musical activities while I was at Merton. I had wanted to find opportunities to play from the time I entered college, but my hopes were fulfilled much earlier than I had expected. I cannot remember exactly when but one morning at breakfast a student sitting next to me chanced to remark that he was studying music. I told him a little nervously that I played the viola and said that I was hoping to be able to play in a chamber-music group. He was a post-graduate student named W; he under-took to find others to join the two of us. On 26 November 1983 we had our first meeting as a quartet in Merton's summer house. On this occasion the first violin part was played by a woman undergraduate from Merton, the second violin was played by W, the 'cello by a woman student from Somerville while I played the viola. I do not remember what piece we played and unfortunately I did not keep a note of it.

As I recall the occasion the other three players were very good. They all asked me what I wanted to play and kindly agreed to perform the piece I selected. We did various repeats of bits which we had not played very well but we worked hard at it and completed all the movements. We began mainly with Haydn, but went on to play pieces by Mozart, Beethoven, Schubert and other composers. We started with quartets such as *The Lark, Fifths* and *The Birds*. We tried various quartets in the *Haydn Set*, composed by Mozart in his middle period. During the year I became pretty busy in my work and could not give much time to playing chamber music.

Early in the New Year I was asked if I would play the viola in a concert sponsored by the MCR. The request came from a woman student at Merton who played the clarinet and who wanted to perform a trio together with another student who played the piano. They needed a viola player to make up the trio and had heard that I played the instrument. I learnt that the piece they wanted to play was a Mozart trio, the *Kegelstatt*.[1] I had heard a recording of this piece, but I had not seen the score and asked for time to consider their request. I really wanted to take part: so I went to a music shop and bought the score. When I read it I came to the conclusion that I could manage it and said that I would take part. We had many practices in Merton's summer house. The piano player took the lead and we worked hard repeating difficult bits over and over or bits where we failed to play in time. I remember even now the way the pianist expressed her approval when we got it right. The concert took place in the Merton's Mure Room on 1 March. Many of my friends came to hear us and almost all the seats were filled. In the second movement the viola has a prominent role but there are some difficult passages. I managed these alright and the third movement went without any problems. I felt relieved that my first concert at Oxford had ended without mishap.

Apart from practising for this concert I continued to practise with the members of the group I have already mentioned. As the girl who played first violin in our group was in her final year and very busy, a don from Brasenose agreed to take over from her. Dr B was doing research on the German composer Spohr.[2] Following the concert in March, especially after the middle of April in the Trinity Term, we

---

[1] Trio for viola, clarinet and piano in E flat, K498
[2] Louis Spohr 1784–1859

78

met as a quartet almost once a week on a Saturday or Sunday morning. If one of the three others was unable to take part in these regular meetings the absentee would generally be responsible for finding a substitute. On the first occasion on which Dr B took part we played Haydn's quartet '*Fifths*' which we had practiced with the others before. I was surprised to hear how well he played. Of course the others also played well. It was very helpful to get his advice on the use of the bow and on playing in time together, but we also got him to suggest pieces which we might play. It was due to him that we played Schubert string quartets and the Brahms' clarinet quintet as well as Spohr string quartets and other works.

I had always been very interested in the string quartets of Mozart and Beethoven and had hoped to be able to play them while I was at Oxford. The others were happy to go along with my wish and almost every week we concentrated on practising a work by one or other composer. We began by playing Beethoven's first quartet, the first of the six in Opus 18. In the last movement of the second quartet in the series there was one point where we all burst out laughing. Interested readers may like to guess where this happened. I recall that we were all quite pleased by our performance of the fourth quartet of the series. From the seventh onwards the quartets became more difficult, but I felt that the depth of sound in these later quartets was special to Beethoven and although they were technically difficult to play they gave me great satisfaction. Of course, we progressed in stops and starts. The eighth is known as the Razumovsky quartet number two; the last movement has to be played by each part at a dizzyingly fast tempo, is full of complicated manoeuvres, and there are places where the parts must not converge. Often in such places I would find to my dismay that I was playing together with someone else's part. I almost felt that I could hear Beethoven laughing. In the ninth, the next quartet, I made another mistake. In this, the third Razumovsky quartet, there is no interval between the third and fourth movements and the fourth movement begins with a solo melody on the viola. The movement is in the form of a fugue and the other instruments take up the theme one by one. This means that the viola part is particularly important at this point. I had not realized this as I had never played the piece before. Towards the end of the third movement I had unfortunately lost my place, and was counting on the interval to find it again, but just when I thought the third movement must have come to an end the other members of the quartet gave me an odd look and B said: 'Hiro, it's your turn to play!'

I would like to mention one more episode in our playing. This happened on one cold day in winter while we were trying to play Haydn's quartet entitled *Seven Last Words on the Cross*. I had brought the score with me. The summer house felt particularly cold that day. This piece, which consists of seven movements, contains many very slow sections, and we were all so cold that after we had played several of the movements, we decided to call it a day. By the way, I have never played this quartet through to the end.

We managed to play all the Beethoven quartets from number one to number eleven, the *Serioso*. Thus, we played all the seventeen quartets up to the four composed in Beethoven's middle period including the quartet entitled *Die Grosse Fugue* (*The Great Fugue*). We played all the quartets by Mozart from his Haydn set onwards with one exception. Haydn composed a huge number of quartets and we had a go at most of those which had been given names. While we were playing one of these B commented: 'In Haydn's music there are elements of modern jazz.' We all nodded in agreement. Among his quartets without names we tried playing Haydn's quartet in F minor, Opus 20, No. 5 and were much impressed by the piece. Apart from works by Beethoven, Mozart and Haydn we greatly enjoyed pieces by Schubert. We began with his *Rosamunde* quartet and on B's recommendation we tried his *Death and the Maiden* quartet. This sounded quite different from Beethoven. We enjoyed the depth of feeling of the music in Schubert's quartet and were tempted to try other pieces by Schubert. B wanted us to try Schubert's quintet with two cellos which Mrs Hall had liked so much, but when I looked at the score I was put off by the length and we never played it while I was at Oxford. When I returned home and did manage to play this wonderful piece I much regretted that I had not played it while at Oxford.

The four of us in the quartet gave some concerts. As on the occasion when I had played in the clarinet trio, the first concert was held in the Mure Room at Merton and we played Dvorak's *America* quartet. We also played Haydn's *Fifths* quartet at Worcester College. I shall never forget the words which W addressed to the audience at the beginning of our performance of the Dvorak quartet: 'This quartet consists of one Japanese and three English members. We are performing the quartet called *America,* a country to which none of us belongs.' The concert at Worcester College took place at lunch-time. A number of students from Merton as well as of Japanese studying at Oxford came along to hear us perform. I was impressed by the fact that white wine was served to all who attended the concert.

Among musical events, other than those to do with chamber music, which I shall not forget is a performance of Handel's *Messiah* held in a church in London as part of the celebrations marking the three-hundredth anniversary of the births of Bach and Handel. This was given by the Oratorio Association of Japan whose concert in Japan had been attended by my mother. Strangely enough, my birthday, which is 23 February, happens to be the same as Handel's. So it was a happy occasion for me that the *Messiah,* which is one of my favourite works and is typical of his compositions, was being performed, in commemoration of the three-hundredth anniversary of his birth, in the country, which he regarded as his second home. The sounds of the music reverberating in the Church were most impressive. I was surprised to see that when the famous *Hallelujah* chorus was reached nearly every member of the audience immediately stood up. This dates back to the time of King George II when the King deeply impressed by the music had stood up at this point. The same Oratorio Association gave another concert in London in September 1985 and visited Oxford where I took part in their performance. In addition to pieces by Handel they played the *Greensleeves Fantasia* (by Vaughan Williams) as well as *Spring Sea*[3] for flute and harp duet. As I was leaving Oxford in the next month I invited Professor Mathias and other dons who had been so helpful to me while I was at Oxford as well as some Oxford friends to the concert. The memory will always remain with me of a moment at the end of the concert when I was asked to stand up for the final piece, *Auld Lang Syne,* which had been selected without my knowledge as a farewell message of good

---

[3] *Spring Sea* is the English for *Haru no umi* composed for *koto* and *shakuhachi* by Miyagi Michio, the blind *koto* player who died in 1956.

wishes. The conductor who made this kind gesture towards me passed away some years ago.

Visit to places associated with musicians: England and music

While I was at Oxford I was able to visit not only many parts of Britain but also a wide variety of countries in Europe including places with musical associations. At Salzburg in Austria I visited the Mozart House where he was born and was kindly allowed to play on the viola which he had used. In Bonn in Germany I visited the house where Beethoven was born. Talking of Beethoven, I shall always remember joining in a performance by the Vienna Philharmonic Orchestra in the Beethoven House on the outskirts of Vienna where Beethoven is said to have written his famous Heiligenstadt Testament. At Prague I visited Dvorak's house where I was allowed to play on his viola and I saw many of his possessions.

Readers may wonder whom I might mention among British composers. In earlier times there were Henry Purcell and John Dowland. Handel lived for a long time in England and readers may recall that there is a memorial to him in Westminster Abbey. As for modern times readers may think of Elgar's *Pomp and Circumstance* and *Love's Greeting*.[4] He was a thorough Englishman, who was born in 1857 and died in 1934. I visited his house in Worcestershire. It was a cosy compact residence where a number of compositions in manuscript together with his violin and various other personal possessions were exhibited. Among these I was very interested to see the huge collection of press cuttings about Elgar which had been collected by his wife who clearly had a mania for collecting. I remember that these were stuck all over the wall. Among English composers dating from after the nineteenth century I should mention among others Britten, Delius and Vaughan Williams. Undoubtedly the Beatles must be added to the pages of musical history while Andrew Lloyd Webber, who wrote the music for *Cats* and *Phantom of the Opera,* may be regarded as representative of modern English composers. His

---

[4] '*Love's Greeting*', the English name for Elgar's *Salute d'Amour*, was composed in 1911 for piano and violin, but later arranged as a string quartet. It also appears as a piece for classical guitar. '

Requiem was composed while I was at Oxford. The author of the Cats poems, the English poet, T. S. Eliot (1888–1965), spent a year at Merton.

So you see, Britain has produced a number of famous composers. Moreover Britain has attracted many foreign composers. Handel spent a long time in England and died there at the end of his long stay. I have already written about Haydn's connections with Oxford. He wrote many of his final symphonies in London. Mozart also came to London and gave a concert there. Mendelssohn was popular in London and earned the trust of Queen Victoria and Prince Albert. Dvorak was awarded an honorary doctorate by Cambridge University and his eighth symphony is known as *England*. Brahms, unfortunately, failed to receive his honorary degree from Cambridge. He had been born in a harbour town but disliked travelling by sea and is said to have refused to travel to England to accept the honour. I do not know whether this is true or not.

However, it seems to me that English people have something of a complex about music in England. They think of Britain as a country which musicians visit and seem to think that their country has not produced many musical figures. My friend W complained that works by English composers were rarely performed, but once when I visited the flat of a friend who was fond of music, I praised a piece of music which he was playing on his tape recorder. This was *Variations on a Theme of Thomas Tallis* by the contemporary composer Vaughan Williams. When I left he lent me the tape, saying: 'I am delighted to be able to introduce works by an English composer to even one more individual who wants to get to know them.' I do not know how far this work is known among music lovers in Japan. It is a marvellous work with a beautiful melody. Probably the work by Vaughan Williams which is best known in Japan is his *Fantasia on the Theme of Greensleeves*. I also like very much his *Lark Ascending*.

Delius came from a German wool merchant's family. He was born in Bradford in Yorkshire but spent more than half of his life outside Britain. As a result some English people do not regard him as an English composer. His music is not always easy to understand, but I think that his *On Hearing the First Cuckoo in Spring*, as well as many of his pieces for wind instruments and strings and his 'cello concerto are superb. Many of Elgar's short pieces for wind and strings are rather plain, but I came to like his first symphony, his 'cello and violin concertos, his piano quintet and his string quartets. I bought a tape of the first symphony in an Oxford record shop and was deeply impressed by it when I listened to it in my rooms in college. I was surprised to discover that a film which I saw at Oxford took this work as its main theme. Apart from these composers I enjoyed Holst's *The Planets,* Britten's *Young People's Guide to the Orchestra,* Walton's viola concerto and music by Howell. [5]

While I was at Oxford I felt that I should get to know and appreciate the music of English composers. So I went to concerts and bought tapes and records. I keep them in my study as treasured souvenirs of my time in England.

I was very fortunate while I was studying at Oxford to be able to see and experience many films, plays and concerts. There are of course also opportunities for me to see performances in Japan, but although Oxford is a comparatively small community there were so many artistic activities close at hand and I was surprised at how easy it was to keep in touch with them. I was fortunate in being able to live for two years in a society where the arts played an easy and natural part in conversation and were an everyday topic.

---

[5] Herbert Howells, born 1892, who succeeded Holst at St Paul's Girls School.

84

CHAPTER 7

SPORT

---□---

Rowing

Beginning with rugby, many sports originated in Britain, and there are lots of British people who enjoy sports on a daily basis. It is amazing how many sports clubs there are at Oxford University. In the town, too, there are many sports facilities. Anyone wanting to take part in sports would find Oxford a well-endowed environment.

Probably the best known sports club in Oxford is the rowing club. The annual boat race between the Oxford and Cambridge clubs has been held ever year since 1829. I was fortunate in being able to watch the race in two consecutive years. The first was in March 1984. On the 17th, the scheduled date of the race, the Cambridge boat, while practising for the race that day, crashed into a barge which was anchored nearby and was badly damaged. As a result, the race was put off until the following day. So I went to the Thames again on the 18th and saw the race from on board another boat. The river banks were crammed with spectators and the shouts of encouragement to the crews never ended. As the Oxford boat went downstream and the river became wider there was a slight curve where there was the usual competition between the two crews to determine which side to take on the curve. Oxford won both the races I saw.

There were rowing clubs in each college. At Merton the crew would be up at six in the morning running and training, I gathered that one of the crew members was inclined to over-sleep; so the other members of the crew would go to his room and wake him up.

When I was invited to the rowing club party in my first term I was asked whether I would like to be their cox, but I declined as I had only rowed a number of times in a four in Japan and had no experience of an eight. However, in my second year I felt that I really would like to row a boat on the Thames. So I asked the captain of the rowing club if I could join in the practice and he willingly agreed. Some days later, I found a rough note in my pigeon hole listing the days, times and place for practice.

The practice began with the crew, which was a mixed one of men and women, carrying the boat out of the boat house. The girl behind me kindly explained how the boat should be carried. The girls in the crew were a really sturdy lot. Even those of slender build had plenty of physical strength. I learnt that there were rules about how you got on board as well as various methods of practising rowing after you were on board. One way was not to move the sliding seats but only use your arms to row; another was to row a number of times with all your strength, followed by several strokes using a little less force. On this occasion the boat captain and the girl I have just mentioned kindly helped me by explaining how it was done. I enjoyed going on the Thames in the boat, but I think that the other members of the crew supported me as a beginner and I realized that it would be difficult for me to become a team member and practise regularly. Moreover, when I was at High School I had found that the oar hit me in the stomach and I had trouble pushing it back. This is popularly called in Japanese *hara-kiri* or cutting the stomach. I wondered what it was called at Oxford; if my memory is correct it is termed 'catching a crab'. The 'Torpid' competition between colleges took place in Hilary Term while 'Eights Week' was held in Trinity Term. In both competitions, which date back to the beginning of the nineteenth century, the aim is to bump into the boat of the other college, hence the term 'bumping races'.

Tennis and Squash

Apart from rowing I particularly enjoyed tennis. I was chosen to play for Merton and thus had the opportunity to take part in competitive matches with other colleges. At the beginning of the Trinity Term in

1984 I received a note from the captain of tennis urging me to take part in 'college practice'. I had met him at MCR parties and on other occasions and as a result we had played many sets together, but I did not know what he meant by the term 'college practice'; out of curiosity I accepted the invitation. 'College practice' took place on the college's lawn tennis courts. I had expected that the practice would involve a lot of hard work and I was surprised by the fact that it simply meant taking part in doubles with other members of the college. But the tennis captain seemed to have watched my play closely and some days later I received a note from him giving the name of my pair as well as instructions on when and where to attend a match and with which college. I remember that I was number three seed in Merton's team of six. The inter-college matches, which generally took place once a week during the Trinity Term in my first year, were played on the lawn tennis (grass) courts which every Oxford college possesses. Merton's courts were near the student quarters belonging to St Catherine's college. There were two hard courts and three grass courts in a corner of the sports ground which faced St Catherine's. I enjoyed playing on grass. There is much less strain on the knees than on a hard court, but at first one had to get used to the way the ball bounces on grass. On a grass court the ball coming towards you seems to slide as it rises. If you are at all careless you are liable to miss the ball or be late with your swing. Even so, once you get used to a grass court it is like nothing on earth, it is so wonderful. The captain of tennis or one of his colleagues told me when and where matches were to take place either through a note in my pigeon-hole or by word of mouth when we met in hall. Singles and doubles matches were decided by the best of three sets. The colleges against which we played were St John's, Worcester, Oriel, Queen's, St Catherine's and Wolfson. I got to know those against whom I played in singles matches and as I mentioned before I even went to concerts together with the player from Queen's. I remember clearly a singles finals match with him which took place on a very hot day when he disappeared to have a drink of water. In the intervals between matches we continued to practise in order to improve coordination with our partner and to get used to playing in lengthy matches. In the end, Merton's performance that year was only fair.

We played hard in our matches, and in true English fashion tea was served in the interval between matches. At tea we did not treat our opponents as enemies, but chatted amicably eating biscuits. However, I was careful not to eat too much when the tea interval occurred between my singles and doubles matches.

Returning to my main theme, I might add that I was particularly struck by the physical strength of my opponents. Therefore, when my opponent combined good technique with physical strength, I often found myself totally defeated. However, even when I was clearly weaker than my opponent, there were times when I returned all the balls using every ounce of strength in my arm and my opponent became tired (or irritated) and lost his poise; I was then eventually able to win the game. Still, I felt a certain handicap in playing against such tall fellows with their powerful serves and strokes.

I have fond memories of the matches against other colleges in which I played for Merton and I shall never forget the many friends I made as a result of playing tennis on grass courts. I recall the face of the captain of tennis who, irrespective of the results, would always say to me after the game: 'Well done Hiro!'

I also had plenty of opportunities of playing tennis other than in college matches. J, the chairman of the MCR, greatly enjoyed tennis and he would invite me and his friends to play on courts not far away from the college on the University sports ground facing Iffley Road. After tennis one day I went with them to a nearby pub where they looked at me wondering who this odd fellow was, but I was glad to lubricate my throat even if I had to admit that the beer was not cold.

I often played with other members of the MCR. There were many tennis enthusiasts in the MCR who would meet in the common room after lunch and decide on the order of play. The level of play varied, but playing tennis, sometimes switching between doubles and singles with different members, is a pleasant way to spend an afternoon. We normally played on Merton courts. As the Merton grass courts were used for official matches I generally only played on them when I was playing for the college and instead used hard courts. On the subject of grass courts I remember an occasion when members of the MCR wanting to use the grass courts were unable to do so. One day when the members met M who, as I have mentioned, became chairman of the MCR in my second year, had a brain wave and proposed that we should use grass courts belonging to other colleges. When we went to a certain college, we found the gate to the court open and it looked as if we could make free use of their court, but only a few minutes after play had commenced a fierce-looking official appeared and I recall that we had to leave the court after we had only been playing for a few minutes.

My tennis friends in the MCR were of various nationalities. In addition to English there were Americans, New Zealanders, Germans, Philippinos and Australians. On Merton courts I usually played with a slightly larger racket. I mentioned, when I wrote about doing my washing, that I had met H, a German. He asked if he could borrow my racket as he thought that there was a greater chance of hitting a ball with a large-sized racket. As I was lucky enough to have two rackets I was able to lend him one. Unfortunately, while he was playing with my racket he hit himself in the face with the racket, perhaps because the ball he was playing had too much top spin. He lost some blood and had to go to the hospital where he needed a number of stitches. Laughing, he said to me: 'It's your fault, Hiro.' Feeling that I did indeed have some responsibility for his mishap I decided to give him the racket as a souvenir. I do not know whether he is still using the racket, but I am sure that he still associates the racket with me and jokes that I brought him bad luck.

On one occasion after tennis we held a barbecue party in the gym nearby. I recall that in my last term at Oxford, when we were all assembled for tennis, someone proposed a party. The sky was cloudy and it looked as if it would rain, but after the game I was able to have my fill of delicious barbecued food. I greatly enjoyed the conversation at the party which was also attended by members of the MCR who did not play tennis.

I would like to relate one other story about tennis. One day, when I was playing singles with one of my Merton doubles partners and managed to win, we got soaked at the end of the set by a sudden rain storm, but we played on and our shirts and hair became sopping wet. We hastened back to Merton; unfortunately, our return coincided with meal time and my college friends, waiting in the queue outside hall and seeing me dripping wet and carrying a racket, teased me by calling out in unison: 'water tennis!' Is this I wonder another English expression?

When I think of tennis in England my thoughts immediately turn to Wimbledon in the summer. I was fortunate in being able to go to Wimbledon on three occasions. The matches I remember best are the singles matches between Connors and McEnroe and Becker and Curren.[1] I had the good fortune to be able to watch the matches sitting next to the Duke of Kent, the President of the club. In the Connors/McEnroe match it seemed to be a one-sided affair with McEnroe in the lead and I remember the Duke muttering: 'Come on Jimmy!' The match between Becker and Curren was also an interesting one. Becker won but I thought his behaviour peculiar. Those concerned with the championship seemed to want Curren to win. The special atmosphere of Wimbledon with its long history lies in the attitudes of the crowd of spectators and reflects, I think, one aspect of Britain. Another English feature of Wimbledon is the serving of tea in the interval. I shall also never forget being able to play tennis twice on grass courts at Wimbledon thanks to the connection I made during my stay with Colonel Hall.

At Merton there is a 'real tennis' court. (This is called '*Le jeu de paume*' in France, 'Court tennis' in America, and 'Royal tennis' in Australia.) 'Real tennis' is the original game as it developed at the court of the King of France under the name '*le jeu de paume*' and spread to England. In Shakespeare's play *Henry V* there is a story of how the Dauphin of France sends King Henry a set of tennis balls.

M happened to know something about 'real tennis' and I was able to play on a number of occasions. The 'real tennis' court was on the other side of Merton Street. The rules of 'real tennis' are frankly complicated and weird. The court is indoors and the shape of a crown is carved on the side wall. Various lines, whose meaning is unclear, are painted on the surface of the court. The net across the centre of the court is the same as in normal tennis. The rackets are narrower and longer than modern tennis rackets and seem to be strung with sheep gut. The ball is roughly the same size as in ordinary

---

[1] In the men's singles at Wimbledon in 1984 John McEnroe (US) beat Jimmy Connors (US) and in 1985 Boris Becker (Germany) beat Kevin Curren (US).

tennis, but is heavy and hard like a baseball. The game begins by the server hitting the ball to a protruding section that looks like a roof, and when the ball hits the ground, the player hits the ball again to continue the game. Points are apparently scored as the ball crosses the centre line. It is also said that points can be gained by hitting the ball into a number of holes [literally depressions] in the side wall. Although I played the game two or three times I never really grasped the rules.

I wonder how many readers understand why in tennis the scoring is 15–0, 30–0 and 40–0. I wondered about the origin of these terms but learnt the answer by chance from one of the Merton dons. According to him the method of scoring in tennis is connected with the counting of time. Fifteen and thirty can be easily understood by looking at a clock, but why forty? He said that forty-five was difficult to pronounce and so forty was chosen. I found this *a* convincing theory. In tennis zero is pronounced 'love'. According to one theory the French used the term *'l'oeuf'* to count zero in *'le jeu de paume,'* since an 0 being a long elliptical shape looks like an egg which in French is *'l'oeuf'*. When the game was brought to England, the English people thought it sounded like 'love' and this word accordingly came to be used in scoring in England. But there are also various other theories including ones which suggest that tennis scoring is related to gambling.

Another game with similarities to tennis is squash. It is also played in an inside court and makes full use of the walls. The rules are not as complicated as in 'real tennis'. The two players face the back wall and play the ball in turns against the four walls making sure that it does not bounce more than once. The ball which is struck hard against the wall may rebound against the back wall and the other player returns it without letting it bounce twice. It is a really tough game. The captain of tennis at Merton was also a very good squash player. When I played with him I soon realized his superior power. When we played together he always stood in the centre of the court and I found myself running all around him and spent my time picking up the ball. Towards the end of the game I felt exhausted but he did not seem a bit tired. I also played with a Canadian member of the MCR but I was beaten. An interesting thing about squash, irrespective of the game itself, is the fact that a red or a yellow mark painted on top of the ball shows the way the ball will bounce. A ball with a red mark will bounce high, one with a yellow mark will have a low bounce. Clearly, the less the ball bounces the more the players have to run. Another interesting fact is that after you have been playing for a bit with a ball with a yellow spot it begins to bounce as if it were alive. I did not play squash as often as I played tennis, but I found that a short time playing squash involved a considerable amount of exercise. I enjoyed playing squash if it was raining and the tennis courts could not be used. Whereas in tennis you use the whole arm, in squash you mainly use the wrist. I do not know whether this was good for my tennis or not, but I thought that strengthening my wrist had benefited my tennis.

Jogging, climbing, skiing and other sporting activities

Jogging was another sport which I enjoyed in my time as a student. Going out from Merton's gate you soon come to Christ Church Meadow. From the entrance it is about two kilometres round the meadow. At one point you come to the banks of the Thames. Jogging there when the weather was fine made one feel good. I often jogged there of an evening and would see the same faces each time. We would exchange greetings but I never discovered their names. Apart from Christ Church Meadow another route on which I also enjoyed jogging was running along the Thames from where Folly Bridge crosses the river on St Aldate's Street as far as Iffley Lock. I shall also refer to this route when speaking of going on a walk with Dr Highfield. From Iffley Lock this route took you near the Church up Iffley Road via the High Street to Merton Street. It was probably about six kilometres in all. It seemed to be good exercise for my police escort who followed me on his bicycle.

Another sport I enjoyed was mountain-climbing. I had done some climbing in Japan and had always dreamt of climbing in Britain. Readers will know that Great Britain consists of England, Scotland, Wales and Northern Ireland, but I expect many would have difficulty in describing the geographical location of mountains in Britain and may even wonder if there are any real mountains in the British Isles.

If you open your map you will see that there is a range of mountains from the centre to the northern part of Scotland and that there are mountains also in the north of England and in North Wales. These mountains are mostly around one thousand metres high, which is roughly the same height as the hills in the Oku-Tama range. As readers will know the highest mountain in Britain is Ben Nevis in Scotland which is 1344 metres high.

From the very day I arrived in Britain I had it in mind to climb the highest mountains in England, Scotland and Wales, but I did not have accurate information about them and much as I wanted to achieve my ambition I was not sure that I would have time to accomplish it. I soon realized that the highest mountain in Britain was in Scotland, but I did not know how high it was or how suitable it was for ordinary climbers. It was in the following summer of 1984 that I managed to climb Ben Nevis. I planned a leisurely trip to Scotland mainly round the north and central part of the country. I found that Ben Nevis attracted many climbers; my police escort told me that if one kept to the normal route it was quite a safe climb and thus my wish to climb Ben Nevis was realized.

The weather was fine on 16 July, the day fixed for the climb. I went by car from Lord Campbell's house near Fort William where I was staying. I was accompanied by a friend of Lord Campbell's son and his wife. From the car Ben Nevis did not look particularly impressive as a mountain but I noticed from the map that there were some steep cliffs at the back of the mountain on the opposite side from the climbers' path. When we got to the beginning of the path I realized that Ben Nevis was indeed a big mountain. Perhaps because it lies in such a northerly latitude there were no wooded areas on its slopes and grass stretched right up to the summit. It became rather cloudy and we could not see the summit which was sheathed in mist. The path had been well maintained and the slope was not too steep, but it was uphill all the way. So it was fortunate that the sun was obscured. We passed various people coming down the mountain and I was interested to hear in addition people talking in German, French and, as I later realized, Danish. After we had passed the lake, which lay half way up, the outlook round about made me realize we had gained considerable height, and I had the same sort of alpine feeling that I get when climbing in Japan's high mountains. After passing a snowy ravine we came to the summit but found ourselves in dense fog and could not see anything. It had taken us just over three hours.

The second mountain, which I climbed on 27 July 1985, was Snowdon, which at 1085 metres is the highest mountain in Wales. There is a small mountain railway that runs up to the summit, but I had made up my mind that I would climb on foot the highest mountains in Scotland, Wales and England. So I climbed up the path which is located on the opposite side of the mountain from the railway track. In contrast to the climb up Ben Nevis, which was a climb straight up the mountain, I felt on this occasion that it was like walking on a ridge. I was spurred on by the sight of the summit with its bare rocks, which I saw from the small lake on the way up, but the climb was easier than that of Ben Nevis and I reached the top easily. The view was obscured by mist and I felt rather depressed when I heard the sound of the train, but I was happy that I had made the climb on my own two feet and appreciated the mountain's comparatively large number of different views. On the way down I followed the path by the railway for part of the way; fortunately, the weather improved and I enjoyed some unexpected views. People waving to me from the train; people looking curious and puzzled; I wonder if I shall see such a sight again.

I went on from Wales to the Lake District where I had been once before. My objective this time was to climb Scafell Pike, which at 978 metres is the highest mountain in England. On 29 July having met up with three fellow students we left our lodgings at Borrowdale to climb to the top of the mountain. The path up the mountain was similar to that up Snowdon, but as we climbed we never seemed to see the summit and I realized that this really was quite a mountain. After we had been climbing for about two hours we came to a beautiful lake where some tents were pitched. Presumably, these belonged to people who were hiking in the mountains. At about this time clouds began to form and hide the mountain tops. When climbing we had occasionally needed to use our hands but it had not been a difficult climb. Threading through the mists we reached the summit in about three-and-a-half hours. The mountain tops appeared and disappeared in the mist and formed a range of rocky mountains. It reminded me of a Japanese mountain range but the biggest difference was probably that, however high you climbed, you kept on encountering sheep.

In this way I managed to climb to the top of the three highest mountains in Britain. I had not been lucky with the weather, but the paths with their ups and downs and the surrounding scenery were different from anything I had experienced in Japan and provided an interesting contrast. British mountains are not particularly high but you get the feeling that you are among high mountains perhaps because Britain lies in such a northerly latitude. There may not be many high mountains in Britain but the country has produced many outstanding mountaineers such as Mallory and Bonnington. Moreover, in the Meiji period it was Walter Weston, the English Missionary, who called Japan's central mountain range 'The Japan Alps' and spread knowledge of Japanese mountains around the world.

I also tried golf on several occasions. I was introduced by one of the dons at Merton to a golf course some fifteen minutes away by car where I had some lessons from a golf pro. It felt good when the impact was right, but I felt pretty wretched when I missed the ball or my club tore up a piece of turf. I am sure that the pro was a good teacher, but I found more attraction in sports where I had to move around more. Nevertheless, I was glad to be able to wield a golf club in Britain, the home of golf.

I suppose that racing should also come under sports! Ascot is famous for racing and I was fortunate in being able to go to 'Royal Ascot' in both 1984 and 1985. It was a colourful occasion. The Queen and members of the Royal Family, who came in horse-driven carriages, were greeted with much applause on their arrival. It was a magnificent sight as those attending doffed their top hats. The Queen is very fond of racing as I could see standing by her side. I was fortunately able to watch the races from the royal box and although I did not understand much about racing I saw the races from start to finish and was overwhelmed by the atmosphere. I noticed that when the Queen entered the enclosure without anyone saying a word a passage was opened to allow her through the throng. I was much impressed by how relaxed the Queen seemed. For the first time in my life I had a bet on a horse race, but it was a spectacular failure. As it was only a one pound bet it did not have any serious effect on my purse.

Winter sports essentially mean skiing. I had the good fortune to be invited two years in succession by Hans Adam, the Crown Prince of Liechtenstein, to stay a few days in his house. From there we could go out skiing not only in Liechtenstein but also in both the Austrian and Swiss Alps. The Crown Prince and his wife Princess Mary had three sons and one daughter. The Crown Prince and his eldest son accompanied me skiing and we all had a relaxing time chatting after our expeditions. On the first occasion a former ski champion who was a member of the police guards for the household of the Prince of Liechtenstein set a course for us to follow and guided me over the course. In the second year temperatures in the Austrian mountains recorded minus 25 degrees centigrade. I was impressed by the extent of European skiing resorts.

I was also invited by the Grand Duke of Luxembourg and his family to stay in their chalet in Switzerland at Cran Montana ski resort and I enjoyed skiing in fresh snow. I thought that the Crown Prince was a very fine skier. I also spent a few days skiing with Colonel Hall and his family at the French ski resort of Meribel. Meribel, which is near Albertville where the winter Olympics were held, is a famous and extensive skiing area. The Halls and I skied around the resort. The area of snow is so vast that one cannot go around it all in one day. I was also able to do some skating on a rink nearby with Colonel Hall's daughter. Afterwards, Colonel Hall said to me more than once: 'I thought that the Prince would stop skiing but I was wrong he was a non-stop skier and I was exhausted.'

I have happy memories of all the sports with which I came in contact during my time studying abroad. Sports often come up in conversation and the fact that I had taken part in sports was often a helpful starting point for a conversation.

With apologies to the English, who regard cricket as their national sport I have to confess that I could not understand the rules of the game. Still, the sight of the players in their white shirts and trousers standing out on the greensward which forms the pitch makes a lovely picture which seems to fit the English landscape. There is something about the cricket bat that makes me think of a rower's oar, and I wonder if it did not have some historical connection with the Vikings. I also wonder what the connections are between cricket and baseball and at this stage I find it more interesting to think about this than to try to understand the rules of cricket.

CHAPTER 8

LIFE AS A RESEARCH
STUDENT AT OXFORD

———————□———————

Why I decided to do research on the Thames as a highway

I have described various aspects of my life at Oxford, but my research was, of course, the most important part of my life there. My two years at Oxford were so precious to me that I did wonder if it would be a waste of time to spend them on the sort of research which I could do in Japan. However, looking back I realize that my research contributed significantly to my experience at Oxford. It certainly enabled me to have many valuable experiences, meet many people and to get the feel of what was involved in research. The theme of my research at Oxford was transport on the river Thames in the eighteenth century. I should first like to explain how I came to study this subject.

From the time when I was a child I had been interested in roads as a means of transportation. In my position I could not go outside the gates whenever I wanted to, but when I wandered along the paths in the grounds of the Akasaka palace, I felt that I was making a journey into a part of the world I did not know at all. For me these paths played an important role as a means of connecting me with the unknown world. It was, I think, when I had only just started school that I found, when wandering around the Akasaka palace grounds, a sign which read '*Ōshū Kaidō*'.[1] The sign was a modern one, but I was excited when

---

[1] The Ōshū Kaidō was an old highway connecting the northern provinces with Edo (now Tokyo).

I learnt that according to old maps and experts on the subject an old highway had indeed passed through the palace grounds during the Kamakura period (1192–1333). Then in my first year at high school when I was reading with my mother Bashō's[2] *Oku no Hosomichi* I became even more interested than I had been before in travels and in transport. Perhaps for this reason my main interest during my first two years at elementary school was learning about the road system and the posting stations along the highways in Edo Japan.

At university I had studied in the history department in the faculty of letters. The focus of my interest gradually moved to the transportation system in the medieval period (from the eleventh century to the end of the sixteenth century) on which little academic research had been carried out. The transportation system in this period developed from the post station[3] system which came into being under the political regime based on the early legal system[4] adapted from Chinese models. It led to the transportation system in the Edo period (1603–1868) of the post-station town[5] system which was developed under the joint shogunate and domain structure.[6] However, as I began my studies I found that there were only a limited number of documents relating to land transport in this period. So I decided to concentrate on the history of sea transport in the Muromachi period (fourteenth to sixteenth centuries) where comparatively more research materials were available. My graduation thesis was a study and analysis of the transport of commodities such as salt, rice, timber and other raw materials in the Inland Sea.

I took up the theme of transport in the Inland Sea in medieval Japan as I had come across some relevant documents. These had been discovered by chance by Mr Hayashiya Tatsusaburo, a Kyoto historian, in a second-hand bookshop in Kyoto about thirty years ago. As I was working on my thesis, I heard from Mr Hayashiya that the papers he had found were going to appear in print. I realized

---

[2] Matsuo Bashō (1644–94) was Japan's foremost haiku poet. *Oku no Hosomichi* describes his journey to the northern provinces.

[3] *Eki-sei* 駅制、

[4] *Ritsuryōsei* 律令制

[5] *shukuekisei* 宿駅制

[6] *bakuhantaisei* 幕藩体制

from my studies at university that research into sea transport in the medieval period had not got very far: fortunately, these documents had come to light just as I was about to take up the theme of sea transport in the Inland Sea. Their publication was most valuable for my research. These documents which were produced in 1445 consisted of the detailed records over one year of duties paid by all shipping entering Hyogo Kitazeki (the northern customs post of Hyogo) which is the modern port of Kobe and which was then part of the domain of the Tōdaiji (temple in Nara). These documents and the customs house records of the port of Lübeck in northern Germany, dating from about the middle of the fourteenth century, are historically important materials. I continued my studies on this theme for about a year as a post-graduate and then I moved to England. There can be no doubt that the methods, which I had learnt in Japan, of how to deal with, read and research historical documents, despite the differences between Japanese and English historical material, stood me in good stead at Oxford.

I decided that, as this was relevant to my previous studies in Japan, I would do research into transport by water in Britain, while I was at Oxford. But when I started at Oxford I had not reached any firm conclusion about the form this should take. English history was outside my special field of study and I realized that it would be far from easy to learn about the background to transport and distribution problems in the period which I wanted to study. I also recognized that research into transport by water in the Middle Ages in Britain, which was related to my studies in Japan, presented particular difficulties as the relevant historical documents in England up to about the seventeenth century were written in Latin and I had never studied Latin. I had, therefore, an immediate problem, as I started my studies at Oxford; how was I was going to read such material in Latin? I only had two years to complete my research and I faced an immediate challenge to the pursuit of my studies.

Professor Mathias

A solution to my problem emerged in discussions with Professor Mathias. As I have already explained Professor Mathias of All Souls had been chosen as my supervisor and Dr Highfield as my college tutor and adviser. Professor Mathias's speciality was the economic history of modern Britain. His work *The First Industrial Nation* has been translated into Japanese and has been widely read as an introduction to modern British economic history. Dr Highfield's speciality was the history of medieval Spain but he was also an expert on the history of Oxford and in 1988, together with Professor Christopher Brooke and Wim Swaan, he published an illustrated book about the buildings and architecture of Oxford and Cambridge. I had been invited to meet both Professor Mathias and Dr Highfield before I had started at Oxford. During my first term I had tutorials with Professor Mathias about historical materials. I went for walks with Dr Highfield and learnt a great deal from him about Oxford by seeing things for myself. All this led me to the study of transport on the river Thames.

In my first term I did not reach any decision on what the exact theme of my research should be. Professor Mathias began by concentrating on a summary of the history of transport in Japan. At his request I wrote an essay outlining the history of transport from ancient times up to the Edo period (1603–1868). Professor Mathias urged me to express more of my own opinions and think about issues such as why horse-driven vehicles were not developed in Japan. This made me apprehensive about how my studies would progress. Apart from my tutorials, I attended Professor Mathias' lectures to learn the general lines of British economic history. Lectures lasted one hour and were given in a not very large classroom in the Examination School and were attended by twenty to thirty finals students. The Professor wore a gown and gave his lecture from a desk on a dais on which he spread his papers. He had an excellent delivery, occasionally writing on the board to explain particular points. With my limited knowledge of English I found it difficult to take in everything he said; so with his permission I brought along a tape-recorder and thus was able to listen again to his lectures back in my rooms. It took time but gradually I began to understand better and this was of benefit to my researches. I also went to similar lectures given by Dr Patrick O'Brien, also of St Anthony's, and attended seminars at the Bodleian Library for students beginning to study history. At these seminars the lecturers, apart from the coordinator, were different each week. The main theme was how to use historical research materials. I found the advice on how to use the Bodleian library particularly useful. Courses of lectures lasted for one term. This did not take place in my first term but I was particularly interested in the course of lectures on the history of Oxford buildings which both Professor Mathias and Dr Highfield urged me to attend. In line with the general thrust of my studies I read books about canals in England, a subject which Professor Mathias knew well and concentrated on expanding my basic knowledge of the subject.

My first term came to an end without my having made a real start with my research. One day after the beginning of my second term I told Professor Mathias that I wanted to study transport on the river Thames. One of the impressions which I had gained from the previous term was that the Thames had played an important role in the transportation of goods within England and I had come to have a real affection for this river which flows through Oxford. I guessed that it should be relatively easy to find in Oxford the necessary historical materials about a river flowing through the city. Professor Mathias, after giving this matter some thought, said that the first problem was to discover how much material there was. As a first step, I should take a look at the historical records, which no one had yet studied, about the toll road which went through Oxfordshire (the Oxford turnpike) in the Oxfordshire County Record Office and then decide how to proceed. When I responded that I particularly wanted to look at transport by water as that was in line with my studies in Japan, Professor Mathias suggested that in that case I should have a look in the Record Office to see what materials there were relating to transport by water.

The County Record Office was in the basement of County Hall a little outside to the west of the centre of the city. Having promised to meet Professor Mathias at the Record Office on a certain day I made my way there. I had no difficulty in finding the hall but I could not discover the entrance to the basement. So I went into the main entrance with my police escort. There I encountered a number of smartly dressed and solemn-looking people and I thought that I must have gone to the wrong entrance by mistake. But one person said: 'I know who you are' and when I asked the way to the basement he kindly told me where to go. Despite the fact that I was wearing jeans I had been recognized. Of course, my visit to the Record Office was entirely a private matter and Professor Mathias had no need to let County Hall know in advance about my visit. I still have a vivid memory of the visit that day. The Record Office was quite light although it was in the basement. I was impressed to see there a variety of individuals including old people, women and obvious students studying the records carefully. I learnt afterwards that ordinary English people are very keen to find out more about the history of their families and that roughly two thirds of those using the Record Office are people looking into their genealogy. Every time I made use of the records in the office I had to enter my name in the visitors' book and explain the purpose of my visit. It was clear from the book that many of the visitors were engaged in genealogical research. In the reading room there were all kinds of information about the various types of records and files held there and where they were to be found. These were piled up in shelves reaching up to the ceiling. Professor Mathias immediately introduced me to the archivist, Mr Burns, who was of great assistance to me in my researches while I was at Oxford and explained to him the nature of my proposed research, asking how much material there was in the record office about the river Thames. Mr Burns disappeared into the back for a moment and shortly after emerged carrying a box nearly a metre long and covered in dust. The box contained a large number of papers relating to the river Thames. The appearance of this dusty commonplace-looking box determined the theme of my two years research at Oxford.

Let me now explain briefly about the Thames. The river has its source in the east-facing slopes of Gloucestershire in the South-West of England. It is 340 kilometres long and after the Severn it is the second longest river in England. The length of the river Thames, by the way, is 30 kilometres shorter than the Shinano River which is the longest river in Japan. Towns on the river going from the estuary towards the source include London, Windsor, famous for Windsor Castle, Henley-on-Thames, where the Henley regatta is held, Reading, Abingdon, Oxford and Lechlade. Many readers will know that London was a Roman city. When the Romans were going up the river Thames the topography of the area and the size of their ships forced them to land where London now lies. As a result, the port of Londinium was developed. According to *A Thames Companion,* written jointly by Mary Pritchard and Humphrey Carpenter, the name of the river derives from the Latin *teme* meaning dark. The Celts, with their religious belief in rivers, found the river Thames, surrounded as it was by marshlands which were difficult to develop, dark and mystical. It must be assumed that this feeling spread among the peoples who arrived there later and led to the Thames being given this name. This is a very interesting theory.

Before I started to read the documents in the Record Office I discussed with Professor Mathias and Mr Burns what particular aspect I should study. It was agreed that I should investigate the facts about the quantities of malt, a raw material for making beer and whisky, transported by boat on the Thames and about the skippers of these boats. I began by reading the records of the Oxfordshire Quarter Sessions. The reason why I studied the transport of malt was that malt was subject to duty. This meant that if any accident occurred which affected the malt in transit on which duty had already been paid the merchants concerned could claim a refund on the portion lost. From the court records I could learn the addresses of the merchants, the amount of malt transported, the places where boats had sunk and other facts about the transport of malt. The records had been preserved because malt was a taxable commodity. As I had decided to research the period from 1750 to 1800, I inevitably concentrated on these records for this period. The records which I looked at were not the originals but copies which had been made in the early twentieth century. As a result, the writing was fortunately easy for me to read. I was not used to eighteenth-century handwriting. So this was a great help to me, but as I progressed I came across places where I thought mistakes had been made in copying and I had to go back to the originals.

Next, I began to do some research in *Jackson's Oxford Journal* in the Bodleian Library. In this weekly local paper I found many interesting articles about topics related to my research. These included the names and numbers of the boatmen and details of the discussions at meetings of the Thames Navigation Commissioners about improvements designed to facilitate navigation and shipping on the Thames as well as information about merchants trading in malt and coal on the river. Fortunately, there was an index in the library covering issues up to 1790. So I was not faced with the laborious task of leafing through quantities of papers to find what I was looking for. Unfortunately, there was no index for the years between 1790 and 1800. So sitting in a separate room in the library I had to go through the papers, which were bound together in a binder and from which clouds of dust rose as I turned the pages, and note down important points on cards. This was a particular chore when I was suffering somewhat from hay fever. I covered the papers up to 1790 in my first year and went through the papers for the remaining ten years in parallel with my other researches. I only finished the last ones shortly before I left Oxford.

I must explain briefly here about the Bodleian Library which was a great boon to Oxford students and researchers. It stemmed from Duke Humfrey's Library which had been built in the latter part of the fifteenth century and which was rebuilt by Sir Thomas Bodley in the seventeenth century. It contains today over fifteen million books and forty thousand manuscripts. I should add that the Bodleian is one of the very few libraries in Britain which automatically receives a copy of every book published in the United Kingdom. Sir Thomas Bodley, the founder of the library, believed that the rule that books should not be taken out of the library should apply to everyone, even the king. As the library contains many old books, photocopies cannot always be obtained and requests are often refused. It took time for a photocopy to be produced even if permission were given. Consequently, you saw many students and researchers in the reading room making notes from books in the library.

To obtain permission to use the Bodleian Library you had to have the approval and recommendation of your supervisor. I recall that in my case the procedures were not at all complicated and permission was given quite readily as I was kindly accompanied by Professor Mathias. I cannot unfortunately now remember the full procedure, but having completed the necessary details on the form I had my photo taken for my permit. My expression in the photo was one of surprise as I looked up towards the bright light shining in my face. But a bigger surprise was that on receiving my permit I was handed a piece of paper covering the rules which must be observed when using the library (such as treating library books with care). Permit-holders were obliged to read these aloud there and then in their own language. In my case I was given a copy of the rules in Japanese which I duly read out. I recall that the Japanese text was not in very good Japanese. This had been, I gathered, the tradition at the Bodleian since the seventeenth century.

Whenever you entered the Bodleian Library you had to show your pass. To search for a book you looked in the huge catalogue in the reading room. The bound volumes of the published index up to 1920 were in one room. The index for later publications was in an adjacent room. So in order to find a book quickly it was necessary to know whether it was published before or after 1920. You could look up books either by the title or by the author's name. There was no problem in consulting a book you were looking for if they were on the open shelves, but if they were in the store you had to complete a form giving details of the book you wanted and hand this in at the desk and wait for it to be brought out. When I was at Oxford the procedure was that the librarian had to fetch each book separately from the store and as this took a comparatively long time I used to order on the previous afternoon the books I wanted to see the following day.

As I have already indicated, the Bodleian Library included sub-sidiary libraries such as the Radcliffe Camera, the New Bodleian Library (referred to below as New Bodleian) and the Science Library. The Radcliffe Camera which was a round building with a large cupola on top in Radcliffe Square could be reached from the Bodleian Library by an underground passage. The New Bodleian was in a building on the other side of Broad Street. Copies of *Jackson's Oxford Journal* which I wanted to consult were held in the New Bodleian.

The first time I went to the New Bodleian I did not realize that you were supposed to check in your belongings and only allowed to take a necessary minimum of items into the library. The doorman was looking down and did not stop me; so I took all my belongings in with me. But, unfortunately, when I came out I was stopped and sternly told that, in future, I must check in my belongings before entering the library. I gathered that pages from old books and documents were sometimes torn out and taken away by readers. Once, when I was collecting my belongings, a student whom I had never seen before said to me: 'I remember how good the food was at Merton.' He must have noticed the magenta Merton scarf I was wearing that day. Each college has a different coloured scarf.

I recall another incident involving the New Bodleian. That was when my umbrella was stolen. It was raining pretty heavily that day, if I remember correctly, and I had gone to the New Bodleian with the umbrella that I had recently bought in London. On the ground floor there was an umbrella rack and I carelessly left my new umbrella there before going upstairs to the reading room to continue my research into *Jackson's Oxford Journal*. When I had finished and went out my umbrella was no longer there. Someone had either taken it by mistake or gone home with it deliberately because it was raining. The rain was coming down harder than ever. When I told the porter that my umbrella was missing he responded: 'What again! I don't know how many times this has happened today!' If it was found he promised to get in touch with me, but there was no hope of my umbrella turning up. Accordingly, I returned to college some ten minutes away through the wet streets and got soaked through. I liked that umbrella and regretted the loss. Whoever had taken it had managed to get home without getting wet, so I reckoned that I had contributed to his welfare. Needless to say, once I was back in my rooms I immediately took a bath.

Apart from items relating to the Thames, there were many other interesting articles in *Jackson's Oxford Journal*. One theme to which I felt like devoting a little time was reading reports of concerts in Oxford. Thus, in my first year, in addition to attending lectures, I spent time in the library and the record office reading the accounts of court proceedings and researching newspaper reports, but by the end of the year I could see the direction in which my studies of the history of transport by water on the river Thames should take.

I had tutorials with Professor Mathias either every week or every other week. His room was on the second floor of the Hawksmoor Tower which had been built to a design by Nicholas Hawksmoor who had been a disciple of Sir Christopher Wren who had designed the Sheldonian. Professor Needham, whom I had met when I had been invited to lunch at All Souls by Professor Mathias before I had started at Merton and while I was staying with the Halls, had rooms on the floor below. There was a sofa near the door of Professor Mathias's room and his desk was at the back. There was a door on the right at the back of the room which seemed to lead to a telephone and typing room. Tutorials took place on the sofa. When I was asked to prepare an essay I would send it to him in advance and the tutorial concentrated on an appraisal of what I had written. As my research progressed and I prepared questions for discussion the tutorial would begin by my making a presentation on which Professor Mathias would comment. He would explain problems in easily understandable language and advise me that on such and such a point I should read a particular book. Occasionally, he would return to his desk to look for a document or book. There were always piles of documents and papers on his desk, but as far as I can remember, with one or two exceptions, he always found what he was looking for. 'I must tidy up' was a phrase I heard Professor Mathias say from time to time during tutorials. The main subjects of my essays were the transport of coal and malt on the river Thames during the eighteenth century. As he wanted me to produce various relevant charts and documents I spent some time searching for the necessary material in the Bodleian Library, the specialist history library immediately on the other side of Broad Street and Merton College library. I could not find a book about the transport of coal that I was looking for even in the specialist history library, but I came across it by chance in the most convenient place of all, namely the college library. I was pleased and relieved when I found the book.

I had collected a good deal of material about the transport of coal and malt on the Thames, but I realized that writing an essay confined to the transport of a single commodity only in relation to the river Thames was not enough. I needed to think about transport of malt in other areas and also about the significance of the transport of such a commodity in the eighteenth century. The knowledge which I could acquire from books was important in this context. At first, I felt that the burden of reading so many books for my tutorials was a heavy one and I needed speed-reading techniques to get through such a huge quantity of books in the limited time available. Of course, it would not do just to cut and paste bits from books. I needed to add my own explanations and opinions. In addition, as I had to write in English the preparation of my essays was a very onerous task.

In the weeks when I had to present an essay I often did not get to sleep until late at night. All my essays were prepared in long hand and it must have been a hard job for Professor Mathias to read them. When I thought that I was getting used to reading quickly and that my essays were getting a little better I was pleased when he said to me: 'This is a much, much better essay than the last one', but then I was disappointed as I realized that the last one must really have been bad and I was rather apprehensive about what he might say about my next effort. After my essay had been looked at critically Professor Mathias invariably gave me directions about the next topic and issues that I should cover. I have to say that although he had described my essay as good he had noted many mistakes in my English. In this way my tutorials and my personal researches were inextricably connected. Although I normally wore jeans, I usually wore a tie when I went for my tutorials. At the end of the tutorial as I said goodbye Professor Mathias would appoint a day and time for my next tutorial. If I had not written an essay that day he would urge me rather sternly to write more quickly, but normally he would say 'good' or 'very good' when he sent me on my way. Often he would treat me to a glass of sherry which he kept in his rooms.

It can be seen from this that my tutorials with Professor Mathias were very substantial but I should point out the differences between my experience at Oxford and the relationship between teacher and student in seminars on medieval Japan in the history department of the faculty of letters in the graduate division of the Gakushūin University. (This was under the direction of Professor Yasuda Motohisa and I shall refer to these as Yasuda seminars.) The Yasuda seminars were attended by second- to fourth-year students specializing in medieval history and the students in each year would form a group and would, for instance, read and discuss a text consisting of a record of the *bakufu* in the Kamakura period. As a result, junior students could always look for help and guidance from senior students in the group. As there were a large variety of aspects to be studied by students specializing in medieval history, Professor Yasuda, who had spent nearly twenty years as a leading teacher in Gakushūin University, had the assistance of sub-teachers who had studied under him. Their task was to help students working on particular themes with which they were familiar. In this way, when the time came for students to write their graduating theses, sub-teachers would come round to the houses where students were staying together to discuss problems and students could be put in touch with seniors who had done research in a similar field. When I came to write my graduating thesis I learnt a good deal about reading and analysing historical texts related to my themes from Professor Yasuda and seniors who had a detailed knowledge about the history of the distribution of commodities as well as from senior students who were not experts in this field. Thus, as a result of attending Yasuda seminars I had a good deal of help and guidance not only from the professor himself but also from seniors in classes above mine and from others who were up to twenty years senior to me.

At Oxford, while I had the benefit of one-to-one tutorials with Professor Mathias in his rooms and from attending his seminars, I did not have contact with senior students of Professor Mathias in the same way as I had had in the Yasuda seminars. Thus, although I gained from thorough man-to-man contacts with my professor I had few opportunities of developing contacts with other scholars and in particular with researchers in related fields. My experience of the Yasuda seminars showed that guidance from the sub-teachers had been very useful. They shared our interest in research and were able to discuss problems which arose in our studies. They also provided good opportunities to meet other researchers in similar fields.

In mid-December, towards the end of my first year at Oxford, Professor Mathias kindly took me to see the Iron Bridge on the river Severn and its museum in North-West Shropshire. The Iron Bridge, which was completed in 1779, was the first bridge in the world made of iron, which as a student of the time of the Industrial Revolution I should not miss. Professor Mathias having given me an account of the bridge then accompanied me to the adjacent museum where he and the museum curator explained the exhibits. We went round the museum, which was in what had been a warehouse, built in 1838, and outside on the site of an iron works, which had continued to operate until the end of the nineteenth century. I was impressed to discover that the first blast furnace, which had been one of the driving forces of the Industrial Revolution, had been preserved. Professor Mathias knew the specialists in economic history throughout the world and, when I visited continental countries, scholars and researchers introduced to me by Professor Mathias guided me to historical sites in their countries. In France, for instance, I was taken to see various canals and in Norway I was shown round the city of Bergen.

In my second year Professor Mathias thought it would be useful if I was able to have the advice of another specialist as well as of himself and suggested Dr Morgan who had studied under him while at New College. Dr Morgan, whose speciality was the history of trade, was then teaching at Bristol University, which lay some 100 kilometres to the west of Oxford. At Professor Mathias's request Dr Morgan agreed to come over from Bristol to give me his advice.

Visiting record offices

Dr Morgan had ginger hair and a somewhat stern face. At first, I did not find him very easy but as we progressed in our talks I realized that he was a good sort. Although he was not an expert in the history of transport by water this was, he said, a good opportunity for him to study the subject. He played the bassoon and was very knowledgeable about music.

The reason why I had chosen to do research into transport on the upper reaches of the Thames was that it was geographically convenient for me while I was studying at Oxford. The Thames passes through the counties of Gloucester, Oxford, Buckingham and Berks before reaching London. So if I wanted to study the upper reaches of the river it would be necessary for me to collect information not only from the record offices and libraries in Oxfordshire but also from offices and libraries in other counties. Whenever he was able to do so Dr Morgan accompanied me on such visits.

The first record office I visited four or five times in the course of my enquiries was at Reading. This was in the corner of a modern building and quite different from the equivalent in Oxford. It was much more spacious and comfortable, but at Oxford the relationship between the users and the archivists was much closer and the atmosphere for research students much better. At this office I looked at the Thames Navigation Commission's report on their investigation into the state of the river and the records of the Berkshire Quarter Sessions in order to find out the state of navigation and the transport of malt on the river Thames at that time. Unfortunately, the record was largely a handwritten one and this made my investigations hard work.

There were also various historical documents in the Gloucestershire record office and library about the upper reaches of the river towards its source. In the latter half of the eighteenth century there was an increase in the transport of goods along canals constructed between rivers. In 1791 the Thames and Severn Canal was completed; this connected the Thames and Severn rivers at Lechlade in Gloucestershire, the highest navigable point on the Thames. The office held many papers, emanating from the Thames and Severn Canal Company, which were very useful for my study of the arrangements for the distribution of commodities in the second half of the eighteenth century. In addition, I found many other papers relating to transport by water.

I also visited the Buckinghamshire record office in Aylesbury, about an hour by car from Oxford, the Public Record Office in London and the Guildhall Library in the City of London. I did not find much of use for my research in the Aylesbury office. In the Guildhall Library I found various insurance company records relating to insurances taken out in respect of the assets and personal property of boatmen and coal merchants and malt traders on the Thames. These were useful in studying the social position of those involved. The records of the Sun Fire Insurance Company had been computerized and were easy to use, but it was a time-consuming task to go through the huge amount of material which had been retained in order to find the facts relating to the people I was studying.

I was always accompanied by one of my two police escorts when I went to these various places. He usually spent his time reading a book which interested him, but he would help me as necessary by noting on cards information about historical documents and assisting me in deciphering difficult passages. As the record office in Reading was in one corner of the county hall there was a cafeteria in the same building. But this was not so at the Guildhall. In this case the chauffeur who had driven me there looked for the nearest pub. Fortunately, he found a good one nearby and every time I visited the Guildhall I went there; it became a favourite of mine. By the way, pub-users in the City of London look quite different from those who go to pubs in Oxford. In the City people in suits and ties, if they cannot find a table to sit at, try to find a space to put down their food and with their beer in their hand talk and laugh – a sight you rarely saw at Oxford.

Dr Morgan told me later on that once when we went to the Guildhall library it seemed that another Japanese researcher was also there at the same time. I had put the name 'Naruhito' on the application form for the document which I wanted to see. The attendant must have thought that this referred to the other oriental person there and saying 'Mr Naruhito' put the papers for which I had applied in front of this man who was greatly disconcerted. However, all the papers which I had requested were delivered to me without a hitch and I was unaware of what had happened. Shortly afterwards, Dr Morgan and Professor Mathias, who were at a conference together, by chance met the Japanese involved. He had seen Dr Morgan by my side and apparently mistaken him for my police escort. What a series of coincidences and rather amusing!

The Public Record Office was in two locations, at Kew and in Chancery Lane in London. The records, which I wanted, were at Kew, but the older ones were in the Chancery Lane office. I also went to the Greater London Record Office for some items. I did not find many relevant documents in the Public Record Office at Kew, but I was interested in the way documents were requested there. You first entered into the computer all the details of the records you were seeking. You then received a pocket-sized receiver. When the documents you required were ready a red light flashed on the receiver and you heard a sound. The receiver thus let you know automatically that your papers could be collected from the desk. The receiver worked wherever you were in the building. In the Greater London Record

Office I was fortunately able to find a paper listing the amount subscribed and the names and occupations of the subscribers to the Thames Navigation Commission; I made a copy of these lists.

In parallel with these investigations I spent some time looking for various documents and records in Oxford. *The Victoria History of the Counties of England,* which contained details of the history of each English county, was very useful in my study of the counties through which the Thames flowed. I also found a number of valuable articles about transport by water. In addition, I discovered that the *Parliamentary Papers* in the basement of the Radcliffe Camera contained some valuable information. Parliamentary approval was required before rivers could be repaired and for the construction of canals. This meant that parliamentary papers were important sources for my study of water transport. I was really surprised how much relevant material there was in these parliamentary records. All the details about the progress of repairs to rivers, about the number of trips made by boats and about the various problems of the river had been recorded. The parliamentary records had been printed and this saved me a great deal of trouble in reading them. I still remember nostalgically the time I spent following the very small print, making notes on cards and inserting onto tables details from these documents; they had a peculiar smell from the store where they had been preserved. *The Universal British Directory* held in the Bodleian Library, which contained the names of merchants active in each place at the time, was also useful to my investigation of those engaged in transport, as well as of merchants involved in the coal and malt trade. When the name Daniel Defoe is mentioned, everyone thinks immediately of *Robinson Crusoe,* but Defoe was a great traveller and in the eighteenth century he went round Britain observing the state of each area of the country. In his account of his travels he recorded among other things the price, means of transport and route taken by coal, as well as details of the trade in malt between Reading and London. I found this most useful. In addition, I discovered the Oxford City Apprentice Records in Oxford City Library; these gave details of the apprentices in eighteenth-century Oxford and were useful for my study of the transport enterprises and malt merchants and their apprentices in Oxford at that time.

I recorded one by one on cards the points which were relevant to my research. At first reading and analysing the records took time, but in this way I made contact with the raw materials of history and I felt happy that I had come in direct touch with the age I was studying through my struggle to read the papers and by breathing in the dust arising from these old papers. I found the officials in the record offices most kind and had the impression that they understood very well how to search out the documents I needed. In particular, I recall how helpful Mr Burns as well as others in the Oxfordshire County Record Office were. He taught me not only how to read difficult words, but was always trying to find where records relating to water transport on the Thames could be found. It would not be an exaggeration to say that every time I went to his office I was able to glean some new information.

Dr Highfield

I cannot record here all the happy memories of my time at Oxford, but my first intellectual excitement after I started at Oxford came from the Oxford historical walks which I did with Dr Highfield who was my college supervisor in college.

Dr Highfield, whose speciality was the medieval history of Spain, was a graduate of Magdalen, but he was also very well informed about English history and recently contributed a forty-page article about early Oxford colleges to the first volume of *The History of Oxford* and, as I have already mentioned, in 1988 he had produced with Professor Brooke and Wim Swaan an illustrated and comparative account of the building of Oxford and Cambridge Universities. This book was in preparation when I was at Oxford. When I was about to leave in the summer of 1985 I often used to see him walking round Oxford accompanied by a photographer.

Dr Highfield, who looked somewhere between fifty and sixty, was a bachelor and lived in college. With his white hair and thick spectacles, and the sly grin he used to give you as you passed him in the street or when he told a joke, there was something special about him which made you think of a wizard riding on a broomstick. As soon as I had joined Merton he used to visit me in my rooms once a week when we would discuss the progress of my studies. Afterwards, we would go out on a walk to look at historical buildings in Oxford. To be honest, when we went on our first walk, I did not realize that this would be the first of some ten historical walks which I would want to record. I thought that he had invited me to go out with him to stretch our legs as a bit of relaxation. However that may be, I must say that through these walks I was able to learn the outlines of the history of Oxford. In addition to the enjoyment gained from seeing the buildings in their historical context I was able to deepen my understanding of the connections between Oxford and my own field study of water transport on the Thames.

My first walk with Dr Highfield was on 15 October 1983. It was pouring with rain and we spent about an hour going round Christ Church meadow. During our walk he explained that the present course of the Thames was different from what it had been in medieval times and that the boundary between Merton and Christ Church Meadow had at that time been part of the city wall. He also told me that the boatmen and boat owners in seventeenth- and eighteenth-century Oxford had lived in an area near Folly Bridge which was not far from the meadow by the Thames. (He had already realized that I had begun to be interested in transport on the river.) As we went along the explanations, which he gave me, aroused my interest in the history of the city of Oxford and of the connections between its inhabitants and the river. I remember clearly to this day the intellectual excitement which I felt at the time. I also recall, after he had warned me to be careful about slipping in the rain, the sight of Dr Highfield making a spectacular fall.

My walks with Dr Highfield took place mainly on Saturdays or Sundays; in my first term alone we took seven walks together. Looking again at my diary to see where we went, I find that on 15 October we went to Christ Church Meadow, on 22 October to the Botanical Gardens and to Magdalen, on 29 October to Queen's, on 5 November to the University Park and to the northern part of Oxford, on 12 November to Worcester [college], on 4 December to Iffley Lock and church, and on 11 December to the neighbourhood of Oxford Castle.

In our walks Dr Highfield did not just comment at random on any old buildings which we passed. He selected two or three and concentrated on the important points about each. I was therefore able to understand without difficulty what he wanted to show me and able to absorb and remember what he said. The following are some examples: the seventeenth-century classical gateway to the Botanical Gardens, the water wheel which is recorded in the eleventh-century Doomsday Book and which lies just above the creek by Magdalen, the plaster work in the ceiling of the library at Queen's, which was completed in the eighteenth century, and in the college chapel, as well as the Baroque gate to the college, the modern buildings of Wolfson by the University Park and the Victorian gothic-style brick buildings of Keble. I remember him saying, as he drew my attention to the pointed entrances and windows in the upper part of these buildings with their peculiarly gothic-style features: 'The gothic-style of the thirteenth to the fifteenth centuries was revived in the Victorian era.'

Before we went to Iffley on 4 December Dr Highfield took me to Merton College library and showed me part of a thick green book and explained: 'Here is the parliamentary resolution of 1624 about the construction of Iffley Lock. The purpose of the lock was to facilitate the transport of stone for building purposes from Headington near Oxford to London and of coal for heating from London to Oxford. On our walk today let us have a look at the lock and the twelfth-century church there.' The documents which he showed me demonstrated that there was no way at that time of getting by barge as far as Oxford and that a great deal of effort had been put into solving this problem.

It was a bright and warm autumn day when we went to Iffley. Dr Highfield carried under his arm a number of volumes about Oxfordshire buildings by Pevsner, the British architectural historian, and walked vigorously along the path by the river Thames as if he was drawn on by invisible forces. I had to make a considerable effort to keep up with his fast pace. I saw then what he had meant by the words when he said on our Christ Church Meadow walk: 'We shall take our exercise walking round the meadow.' At the same time I realized that the speed with which he walked reflected his passion for scholarship which I began to share.

Iffley Lock lay below a small hill in beautiful country. At today's newly renovated lock there were a number of leisure boats and people chatting amiably waiting before the lock gates for the lock to open. There was no sign now of the difficulties which had faced earlier navigators on the river or of the efforts which had been expended in building the lock. But it was very useful for my later studies to see with my own eyes how the lock operated. We crossed over the lock and went towards the church. There were few vehicles on the quiet paved road up to the church. The church blended in with the old buildings around and the general atmosphere made me think of the Middle Ages. The church was on top of the hill. It was a symmetrical and elegant small building. I liked this building as soon as I saw it. The doorway at the front of the building with its Norman decoration was so well preserved that one could hardly believe that it had been built in the twelfth century. Dr Highfield explained in detail about round Norman arches and the decorations surrounding doors. It was an unforgettable walk which had taken us to this ancient and fine twelfth-century church.

On our final walk that first term Dr Highfield took me to Oxford Castle. Oxford Castle had been built in 1071 five years after the Norman Conquest by Robert d'Oilly who had been appointed governor of Oxford by William the Conqueror. As the castle is now within the precincts of Oxford prison it is not open to the general public, but we were able to get a general view of it from the path which follows the stream beside the castle. Dr Highfield pointed out that there used to be a water wheel standing just below the tower and mound which were all that remain of the old castle today, and as we moved south along the creek he said that this area was called Fisher Row and was the second of two areas where those engaged in the carriage of goods had lived (the other area being by Folly Bridge). Finally, he noted that Oxford prison was in the precincts of the castle and commented with a laugh: 'You see the castle's role has not changed in over a thousand years!'

The first time I was invited by Dr Highfield for tea in his room was shortly after I had begun my stay with Colonel and Mrs Hall to improve my knowledge of English. I shall never forget my first impression of him as he greeted me. He was standing erect in a dark blue suit with piercing but kindly-looking eyes peering through thick spectacles and raised his hand to welcome me. Sitting me on the sofa by the window he showed me a book and said that he thought I might find it useful to glance through the book before I began my studies at Oxford. This was an outline history by J.H. Clapham of the economic history of England in the Middle Ages. It dealt with a period before the eighteenth century, which I was proposing to study, but the section about transport in the Middle Ages was very useful for my later studies. Dr Highfield, putting an electric lead into an ancient and battered electric kettle, began to make tea. While Colonel Hall was discussing with Dr Highfield how I was getting on with my language studies and what the next steps should be, the kettle in which the water had boiled began to spew out steam as if it was about to explode. Somewhat scared, I moved away from the kettle, but Dr Highfield was obviously used to the ways of his kettle and, removing the cord, put in the tea. It was very delicious tea. As I was finishing my tea he asked me if I would like to hear a record and while waiting for me to reply put on a record of Haydn's *Military Symphony*. His record-player looked as old as his electric kettle, but the sound reproduction was good.

After I entered college I used to visit Dr Highfield's room in connection with the essays which I had to prepare for presentation to Professor Mathias. He readily replied to all my trifling questions and produced relevant papers for me to look at. When he could not give an immediate response he would make a memo of the details I wanted and would put his reply in my college pigeon hole. Sometimes, if he came across things which might be relevant to my studies, he would follow the same procedure. Unfortunately, however, I found his handwriting very difficult to read and occasionally I had to seek the assistance of my police escort, but trying to read his handwriting was good practice for my reading of hand-written historical documents, which I had to look at in the course of my researches.

Among the happy memories of my association with Dr Highfield were the visits we made to operas together. The first of the operas we saw was Beethoven's *Fidelio* on 26 October. There was a scene at the beginning of the opera when a woman was ironing; it looked just like the ironing we did at college, and struck me as funny. It was a good performance but it seemed rather a gloomy opera. This was the first time I had been to an opera in England. The last opera, which

I saw with Dr Highfield, was *The Marriage of Figaro* in a fine production at Glyndebourne; it left a deep impression on me. People with whom I went to operas while I was at Oxford were Mrs Storry (wife and later widow of Richard Storry, the outstanding and irreplaceable scholar of Japanese at Oxford), Mr and Mrs Fuji and my police escort. I greatly enjoyed opera; this was a great boon from my stay in Oxford.

After the opera I usually had a meal with Dr Highfield. We had supper in a cosy and very quiet room, down some stairs, a little below the rooms occupied by Merton dons. Drinking wine (the Spanish wine we drank after *The Marriage of Figaro* was especially good) we talked until late about the opera we had seen.

I cannot record here all my happy memories of Dr Highfield, but I made one major blunder in my relations with him. It happened when we were taking one of our walks in Oxford. Generally at the end of our walk we discussed when and where our next walk should take place. On one walk both I and my police escort failed to note this down in our notebooks. The day in question happened to be that on which the Oxford Colleges boat races took place and I had gone to the Thames to watch them. It was some time after three in the afternoon when I returned to the porter's lodge and looking in my pigeon hole saw a memo in Dr Highfield's handwriting saying that he had been waiting at the lodge from two o'clock. I was greatly embarrassed and immediately went round to his rooms. He did not seem in the least put out and when I apologized for forgetting our appointment, saying that I had gone to watch the boat races, he responded gently: 'I thought that you might have gone to see the races. They are an important tradition at Oxford and it was a good idea to watch them.' As I could not think of anything to say in reply I quickly left his rooms after promising that I would not make such a mistake again in the future. I still feel guilty that I had wasted his precious time; I knew that in his capacity as a tutor he had many students to supervise and that this left him little time for his own researches, but I was somewhat relieved by the thought that it had been the boat races which I had been to see on that occasion.

Among my memories of Dr Highfield I recall the time when in my last summer we visited the upper reaches of the Thames and the

Thames and Severn canal. We first looked at three bridges across the upper reaches of the river. The first one was called 'New Bridge', but the adjective new was far from appropriate in this case, as it was an old bridge built in the fourteenth to the fifteenth century. I wonder if it was called 'new' much in the same way as New College was so termed. Dr Highfield explained that the stone used to build this bridge had come from the Cotswold Hills which extend from the western part of Oxfordshire as far as the eastern part of Gloucestershire. The next was 'Tadpole Bridge' but no one apparently knows why it was so called. The last was 'Radcot Bridge' which was also said to have been built in the fourteenth century and, according to Dr Highfield, Cotswold stones had also been used in its construction. Our next objective was Grafton Lock some kilometres upstream, but he suggested that instead of using the car we walk along the path by the river. However, it was further than it appeared from the map and the grass was growing high beside the path. Eventually, we managed to push through the grass thickets and reached the lock, although in the process we suffered from the sharp pricks of the grass.

The lock-keeper kindly agreed to show us round and let us see some photographs of the floods which had swamped the area some years earlier. Dr Highfield, feeling perhaps that he had been responsible for forcing us to go through the 'jungle' on our way to the lock, decided to go back the same way with the driver to collect the car from Radcot Bridge and he left me and my police escort at the lock. Having seen them off I heard more about the floods from the lock-keeper. While we were talking, a boat came down the river and at the suggestion of the lock-keeper I and my police escort joined the boat as far as Radcot Bridge and set off in pursuit of Dr Highfield and the driver. The boat contained a couple who were going down the Thames as far as London. We spotted Dr Highfield and the driver some distance away and shouted after them, but we were too far away for them to hear us. As I have mentioned earlier, Dr Highfield keeps up a fast pace and our hopes of reaching Radcot Bridge by the time they did so were dashed. When we reached the bridge we found that he and the driver had already left by car to pick us up at the lock. I remember that we had to wait a few minutes before they appeared again at the bridge. I remember it did not take more than a few minutes before the smiling face of Dr Highfield appeared again at the bridge.

After we had had lunch at Cirencester we went to look at the Thames and Severn canal which had been shut at the beginning of the twentieth century and has turned into stagnant pools of water. I could not help feeling sad at the contrast between the vitality of the surrounding green fields and the canal which no longer had any life. I must mention the Sapperton Tunnel which was over three kilometres in length and was opened in 1789. The entrance to the tunnel with its fine stone construction reflected the combined technical skills of the time. I was impressed by the self-confidence of those involved in the construction. Dr Highfield made some very interesting comments here. He pointed out that the tunnel, which had been constructed, was too narrow for the horses, which had pulled the barges, to enter; so the boatmen lying down on boards placed across their boats would propel the boat forward by pushing their feet against the ceiling and side walls of the tunnel. In other words, the boats were propelled by human feet. He pointed out a pub which stood near the entrance to the tunnel and explained that, while the boatmen were struggling to push their boats through the tunnel, the horses and their drivers would take the road above the tunnel to the other end and then spend the time in the pub until the boats appeared. No doubt this was why there was a pub at both ends of the tunnel. But it does seem to me that they showed rather a lack of fellow feeling by passing the time having a drink while their companions were struggling away inside the tunnel.

After we had had a look at the tunnel we went to see the source of the Thames but unfortunately the water had dried up and we were unable to see where the river started. Our last stop that day was at Lechlade where we looked at St John's Lock which is the highest lock on the Thames. There was a stone monument by the side of the lock, which had originally been at the Crystal Palace in London and had been moved to the source of the Thames. According to the plate on the lower part of the monument it had been moved there in 1974. A number of leisure boats arrived at the lock while we were there and the lock-keeper had a busy time opening and shutting the lock. The people on the boats looked relaxed. In the background I could see the small tower of a pretty-looking church on the other side of a meadow. This was undoubtedly the highlight of our seven-hour tour that day.

I learnt a great deal over my two years in Oxford from Dr Highfield. He taught me so much during our walks about the history of Oxford, helped me in so many ways while preparing my essays, accompanied me to the opera and took me to the upper reaches of the Thames. His influence on me has been incalculable. Dr Highfield was in every meaning of the word my 'moral tutor' in guiding me through the difficulties, hardships and joys of the pursuit of learning.

Preparing my thesis[7]

Based on the historical materials which I had collected during my two years at Oxford I analysed the state of water transport on the Thames, concentrating on the people who had been involved in improvements to the river and navigation on it, and on the transport of agricultural commodities including coal and malt. The following is a brief outline of my dissertation.

Generally speaking, English people in the Middle Ages were more interested in using rivers to help them to live rather than as transport routes. As a result, rivers were dammed to provide traps for fishermen and waterwheels for millers of corn. This led to endless disputes between those whose primary interest was in the dams and fish traps and those who wanted to use their boats on the rivers; the Thames was no exception.

In the thirteenth century a compromise was reached between those engaged in the carrying trade and the millers leading to what were called 'flash locks'. These were movable water gates which allowed boats to pass through the dams, which I have just mentioned, but the boatmen had to struggle hard to prevent their vessels from capsizing in the fast flowing and turbulent waters when the gates were opened. There were a number of incidents of boats

---

[7] This was produced as *The Thames as Highway, A Study of Navigation and Traffic on the Upper Thames in the Eighteenth Century* by H.I.H. Prince Naruhito and printed at the Oxford University Press Printing House in 1989.

capsizing. The millers also needed time for water levels to rise sufficiently so that their water wheels would work properly again.

In the seventeenth and eighteenth centuries the expansion of London and the development of agriculture in the surrounding area led to increasing importance being attached to rivers as highways. The technical innovation of 'pound locks', contributed to a solution of the disputes between the millers and those engaged in transport. You will still find many examples of this type of lock on rivers and canals. 'The pound lock consists of a chamber, made of bricks and stones, enclosed within two sets of gates fitted with two sluices. A boat enters the chamber to go downstream. The gates are shut and the water is drained from the chamber through sluices in the lower gates, till the water inside is equal to that outside. Then the lower gates are shut and the lock chamber is filled with water entering through sluices in the upper gate.'[8] As a result of the invention of the 'pound lock' boats were able to move up and down from fast-flowing sections of the river without displacing large amounts of water. The Thames Navigation Commission which was established in the middle of the eighteenth century carried out a series of improvements to the river, including the construction of 'pound locks', designed to speed up transport on the river. During the 1790s – the so-called era of canal mania – various canals were built with junctions to the Thames. This led to significant changes in the nature of transport of commodities on the river. I added as an example of these changes some observations on the Thames and Severn canal.

I realized that as a result of various improvements made to the river there had been a striking increase in the quantities of commodities transported on the river, a decrease in accidents to boats following the construction of 'pound locks' and a reduction in tariffs for the transport of commodities. The average tonnage of boats on the Thames at that time was seventy to eighty tons. Although 'pound locks' had come into widespread use, the boatmen still faced problems in passing through the remaining 'flash locks'. When there was a drought there would not be enough water and when there were

---

[8] Quotation from C. Hadfield *British Canals*, Newton Abbott, 1984, page 22.

floods there would be too much; these conditions hindered navigation. The Thames and Severn Canal Company owned boats of their own which participated in navigation on the rivers.

The transport of coal on the river Thames was very important. The Thames Navigation Commission set the tolls for transporting coal and the contribution to be made towards improvements to the river. At the beginning of the eighteenth century the river was used to transport coal to Oxford from London, to which it had been brought from Newcastle. But towards the end of the eighteenth century coal from Wales and the Midlands could be transported more cheaply to Oxford via the Thames and Severn Canal and via the Oxford Canal which connected the neighbourhood of Birmingham with the Thames. This led to fierce price competition and gradually coal from Newcastle was displaced. Generally, merchants who dealt in coal were not simply coal merchants but combined the business with dealing in various other commodities such as timber. I found many interesting records about these merchants as well as about those engaged in transport business. The fact that they mostly lived in the vicinity of the river was due to its being convenient for their trades.

The transport of agricultural commodities was as important as that of coal. The most important commodities were grains including malt for use in brewing beer. Prior to the construction of canals these commodities had followed the opposite course to that of coal, going down stream to London. But the development of canals facilitated the exchange of commodities between London and the mid-western part of England via the Thames. According to the records, unlike the coal merchants who lived near the Thames, the malt merchants lived in a wider area. As a result, they used horse- or hand-driven carts to carry malt to the nearest river. The transport of malt was seasonal and influenced by the appropriate time for brewing, the winter being the most important season.

Let us take a quick look at the transport of commodities other than coal and malt up the Thames from London. I was surprised to find how many different commodities had been carried by boats belonging to the Thames and Severn Canal Company in the period between September 1794 and the end of 1797. Apart from a number of agricultural products I found thirty-five different items including a variety of manufactured goods such as metal products, dye-stuffs presumably for use in making textiles, alum, cider, wine, ale and other alcoholic beverages except rum, items from the colonies including sugar, tobacco, rice and tea, as well as stone, and timber. This made me realize what a huge trading centre London was. But it was interesting that there was no reference in the statistics to coffee, which was beginning to be appreciated in England, but was presumably not yet a popular drink. Among manufactured goods there were items which seemed to have come from Scandinavia and countries on the Baltic Sea. Together with the many items originating in the colonies they painted a picture of London as an international city.

The above is a rough sketch of my thesis. I was very pleased that recently it has been produced under the title of *The Thames as Highway* under the imprint of Oxford University Press. I shall never forget the help I received from so many people, especially Professor Mathias and Dr Highfield. When I returned to Japan and was organizing the results of my research, I recognized once again the assistance, which I had received in my researches, from the well-stocked British libraries and record offices and from their respective archivists. They have, without doubt, made a significant contribution to the high level attained by English historical research. When I re-read *The Thames as Highway* I relive my days by the Thames. Apart from all my efforts to collect records about the river I recall so many happy moments – my walks beside the river with Dr Highfield, the sights of the softly flowing Thames and the beautiful landscape around the river, which helped to cure the weariness resulting from my studies, the days on which I jogged beside the river and the times when from the top of the boat house I watched enthusiastically the college boat races. It is seven years since I left Oxford and even though the river is on the other side of the globe the name of the Thames conjures up in me feelings of affection and nostalgia transcending distance and time. While I was at Oxford the Thames was the prop of my life and of my studies. I dearly wish that I could see the river again with my own eyes and re-live the happy days of my youth beside the Thames.

Canals past and future

From the standpoint of the history of transport since the eighteenth century, I should like to add a few words, about how the Thames has changed. The coming of the railway age in the nineteenth-century had a huge impact on river and canal transport including transport on the Thames. The first railway in England was completed between Stockton and Darlington in 1825 and coal could be transported from the inland Durham coal fields to the coast. The railway between Liverpool and Manchester opened in 1830 and marked the real beginning of the railway age, but the construction of railways did not lead to the immediate demise of canals. According to parliamentary papers pottery and china were being transported via the Oxford canal in the middle of the nineteenth century; breakable items were carried on canal boats rather than by rail. By the 1860s commodities, particularly coal, were generally transported by rail. After the First World War commodities began to be moved by lorry and the role of canals in the transport of commodities came to an end. As a result, many canals, which had hitherto been prosperous, were closed and the water ceased to flow in them. The sight in these days of fishermen with rod and line fishing in the 'pound lock' pools shows how far canals have declined from their past prosperity. But in recent years canals have developed into leisure facilities for pleasure boats and many canals, which had been shut, have been revived for leisure purposes. Moreover, as water supplies become increasingly strained, proposals have emerged for canals to be used to carry water from areas of plenty such as North Wales to those where water is in short supply. The cost of making an existing canal usable is about one tenth of that of laying a pipe line while the operational cost is about one seventh. The construction is said to be fairly simple involving the placing of pumps at key points to change the direction of water flow. Canals, which were one of the important products of the Industrial Revolution, are finding new uses these days and being revived for leisure purposes or for water supply.

In Europe the Rhine, Main, Danube Canal was completed in September 1992, thus linking the three rivers and providing a means of moving commodities from the North Sea to the Black Sea.

The countries through which the route passes are from the North, Holland, Germany, Austria, Czechoslovakia[9] and Hungary, Yugoslavia, Rumania, Bulgaria, and Moldavia (which was part of the former Soviet Union), thus linking Western and Eastern Europe. Today when relations between Eastern European countries and those in Western Europe are becoming closer it has an important role to play in bringing the economically advanced and the less developed areas closer together. This year [1992] marks the completion of the European single market. I shall be very interested to see how canals are used in the future.

---

[9] At the time the Prince was writing the Czech Republic and Slovakia had not become independent states.

CHAPTER 9

TRAVELS IN BRITAIN AND ABROAD

———————□———————

Weekend drives in the countryside around Oxford

During my two years at Oxford I managed to travel a good deal in Britain and Europe. I propose to begin by describing some weekend drives I made in the neighbourhood of Oxford. As, of course, I did not have a driving licence, I arranged for my police escort to be my driver. Sometimes he and I went out on our own; on other occasions I took Oxford friends with me.

On many weekends I went into the Cotswolds which stretch from the north-west of Oxford to the neighbouring county of Gloucestershire. When I looked from a high point with a wide view of the countryside I could see the beautiful Cotswold villages – groups of the local honey-coloured stone houses clustered around church towers.

Burford on the western fringe of Oxfordshire, with its gently sloping High Street and attractive buildings on each side was beautiful, and I was attracted by the town of Bibury in Gloucestershire on the way from Burford to Cirencester. I was interested in the differing shades of the honey-coloured stone with which the houses in the various villages on the way were built, and Bourton-on-the-Water with its houses reflected in the river had a charm of its own.

Cirencester was a Roman town. Most towns whose names end in 'cester' or 'chester' trace their origin to Roman times. Chester in the north of England, Winchester and Dorchester in the south were said to have been Roman garrison towns. The roads which meet at

Cirencester were mainly straight roads. It is well known that the Romans built straight roads in order to facilitate the transmission of information and the speedy movement of their troops. The sayings 'all roads lead to Rome' and 'Rome is eternal' are well known. When I looked at these straight roads and saw that these Roman roads were still being used today, was it a hasty conclusion to think that they had indeed preserved an eternal life? I had once visited Cirencester on a cold winter's day. After having a look at the town and while I was looking for the remains of the Roman theatre I came across a mound. There was a depression in the middle of the mound and children were tobogganing on the slopes where there was still some snow. This was where the Roman theatre had been. There was no hint here of 'eternal Rome'; I could only feel the loneliness and emptiness of the place.

On the borders of south-west Oxfordshire and Wiltshire there is a huge image of a white horse carved into the chalk slopes of a hill. According to one theory, it originated in the time of King Alfred around the ninth century. It must have been a huge job to create it. You can walk over parts of the horse on the upper part of the hill; as you find your way the horse seems so big that it is even difficult to estimate what part you are standing on. I visited this spot twice. On the first occasion there was a heavy rain storm; on the second it was a fine day and I was able to see clearly from quite far away the whole shape of the white horse. But, as I gazed at it this time I thought that although it did look like a horse, it could also be some other kind of unknown animal. There are various other white horses elsewhere but I was told that this was the oldest of them all.

The visits which I made to towns and villages on the Thames were interesting. I particularly enjoyed drives and walks on the banks of the river from Wallingford, south of Oxford, to Goring and Henley. There were many attractive places near Oxford to visit at weekends but I cannot describe them all. If I had passed my time at Oxford without seeing these places I should have been like a man who remained in 'the dark spot under the lighthouse',[1] so I made every effort to explore the area round Oxford.

---

[1] The Prince was quoting a famous Japanese proverb *Tōdai moto kurashi*.

Trips in Britain involving overnight stays

The first time I stayed away anywhere in Britain was in December of my first year when I visited Broughton Castle. I spent some days staying with Lord and Lady Saye and Sele and again experienced the warmth of English family life. Broughton is a beautiful castle surrounded by a moat. It is magnificent both inside and out. Lady Saye was a viola player and we played duets. Neighbours came round and we sang carols. As a result of this visit, when my parents visited England in the following year, they stayed at Broughton.

That same month I visited Cambridge which is also a university town, but in Cambridge the colleges are closer together and I had the impression that it is more of a university town than Oxford. I thought that the gently sloping lawns down to the river Cam with the colleges in the background were especially attractive. I had particularly wanted to visit Kings College Chapel but, unfortunately, as this coincided with the middle of a recording session, this was not possible.

In the latter part of December I visited Chester and York in the north of England. They are both fine walled cities. In Chester there are remains from Roman times all over the place. York was so named after the Viking conqueror Jorvic and a Viking museum was under construction there. York Minister is a huge white cathedral, whose dignified grandeur cannot be easily described and which I found overwhelming. I climbed up the staircase to the top of the cathedral; it was a long climb and I was quite out of breath. There was a superb view of the Minster from on top of the walls. The atmosphere of the narrow streets of the city and the surrounding buildings created a feeling that one was back in medieval times. I found strolling round the city most enjoyable.

There were many other places in Britain where history seemed still alive. For someone who had studied medieval history in Japan, as I had done, it was exciting to walk round these historical towns with their savour of olden times and shadows of the past; it seemed like travelling in a time machine. I felt much the same excitement when I visited Prague in Czechoslovakia and old towns in Italy, such as Siena and Orvieto. There are also historical towns in Japan but

I do not think that they convey as a whole quite the same feeling of being back in a past age.

In 1984, I spent nine days in Cornwall in the south-west of England. Although it was only April, I felt immediately that the sun was stronger there. Someone from an aristocratic family, whom I had met soon after I started at Oxford, introduced me to some families who were living there and while staying with them I made various trips. At the house of the Galsworthys near Truro I was shown a magnificent garden. The camellias were particularly fine. There were also many precious books in this house. When after a meal I asked a question the host would suddenly disappear, and then reappear with a large volume and proceed to answer my question. They were a very pleasant couple and I had a relaxing two days with them.

In June I went to Liverpool in the north-west of England in order to be present at the opening ceremony for a Japanese Garden. Liverpool was the home base from which the Beatles overwhelmed the world. I visited the museum devoted to their memory and listening to the deeply familiar beat I took a trip down memory lane.

In July I made a long tour of eleven days to Scotland. I spent most of the time in the Highlands, but I also went over to the Shetlands, the most northerly islands in Britain. There were no trees there that could really be called trees, but I saw some Viking dwellings called brochs[2] which looked as though they were the result of haphazardly piling up stones. This place made me feel that I had come to the most deserted and lonely spot at the northern tip of the country. As in Helsinki, the capital of Finland, which is on the same latitude, it was still so light at midnight that one could read a newspaper. By the way, when I asked in the Shetlands what was the nearest place the reply was 'Norway'.

Returning to the mainland of Scotland I went to Glencoe and Loch Ness. Here I was looked after by Lord Campbell whom I have already mentioned. Talking with Lord Campbell's family and representatives of other clans in various parts of Scotland I could not help noting their resentment and the grudge they bore towards

---

[2] A broch according to the OED is 'in Scotland a prehistoric stone tower'.

England, because, half-defeated by the English, they had not been able to adopt a direct descendant of the Stuarts as their king in succession to the English king. How many times did I not hear on this journey the remark 'The English destroyed everything!' The Campbells liked to sing 'The Skye Boat Song'. This was a song in which there was a touch of sadness and told the story of how Bonny Prince Charlie, the descendant of the Stuart King James I (formerly King James VI of Scotland), had been forced to flee to the Island of Skye although he had been born a royal prince. I could not avoid noting in their expressions, as they sang, their feelings, which cannot be easily put into words, of affection for their homeland of Scotland and for Prince Charlie. Scotland is part of the United Kingdom but retains its own currency[3] and Scottish banks print their own notes and mint their own coins.

I was again in Scotland that September when I had the good fortune to be invited to spend a few days with the Queen and Prince Philip at Balmoral near Aberdeen. I was much impressed by the way they enjoyed their holidays in the wide open spaces around Balmoral.

In March 1985 I visited South Wales. I was surprised to see that, when the train reached Newport, which was the first station in Wales, the names of the stations were in Welsh as well as in English. On this occasion I only visited the southern part of the Principality, but I found the Welsh kindly people and felt a different sort of warmth there than I had felt in England and Scotland. The Welsh are famous for their love of singing and they naturally break into song on every sort of occasion. I joined in several times. I went on by train to Durham in northern England to attend a world kendo championship meeting. Looking out of the train window on arrival the sight of the cathedral towering up above the city was stunning.

In April I went to Lincoln in the east of England. The daffodils were blooming in the gardens of Doddington Hall outside Lincoln. I shall also never forget the beauty of Lincoln cathedral. After I had met the Mayor of Lincoln at the Guildhall I went on towards Peterborough stopping for lunch at the George Inn at Stamford as

---

[3] While Scottish banks still issue their own notes and there are a few Scottish coins there is no separate Scottish currency.

recommended by Professor Mathias. On the following day I travelled on from Peterborough to Norwich. Norwich is an example of an English medieval city; the stone cobbled road up to Elm Hill in the middle of the city had a medieval feel about it. I had a guide who showed me round; it was interesting the way in which he kept on talking about places that were haunted by ghosts as if this was the most natural thing in the world.

In June at the beginning of the long university summer holiday I visited the University of Essex.[4] In the neighbourhood I also visited the River Stour, which is famous for the paintings of the Hay Wain and the watermill[5] by Constable, the outstanding nineteenth-century artist. It was raining that day but this made the greenery more vivid and beautiful.

In July Lord Cranborne whom I had got to know invited me to stay. I spent a pleasant day with the Cranbornes playing various sports and enjoying other activities. That month I also went to the south-east of England visiting Dover among other places. I saw the famous white cliffs of Dover and was impressed by the construction of Dover castle and the beautiful medieval town of Rye. I shall also not forget the three days I spent that month staying with Sir Peter Miller, the Chairman of Lloyds Insurance, at his house on the Channel Island of Sark. There are no cars on the island. The only means of transport are tractors, horse-drawn carriages and bicycles. We naturally went round on bicycles. For the first time, I also had the experience of diving in a wet suit. In August, I visited Portsmouth and the Isle of Wight among other places in the south of England. I really did get round quite a bit!

While I was at Oxford I stayed at a 'Bed and Breakfast' in the neighbourhood. Many people will have seen notice-boards advertising B and Bs as they are called. In B and Bs ordinary people offer a bedroom in which guests can stay and provide breakfast the following morning. These are the English equivalent of Japanese *minshuku*. When I arrived there in the evening the lady of the house showed

---

[4] The University of Essex was established in 1965. When the Prince visited the university it had just opened a department for Japanese studies.
[5] Flatford Mill.

me to my room and politely explained to me how to use the shower. After this she told me where I could find a television set if I wanted to watch TV. And having told me to make myself comfortable she disappeared into another part of the house. The landlady did not, of course, know who I was. My police escort made sure of this. For breakfast the following day I had a plate of delicious bacon and eggs, far tastier than what you would get in a hotel. I put 'Hiro' as my name down in the visitors book and returned to Oxford.

I must add one other thing. In my visits to English manor houses I came across many places which had lots of Chinese and Japanese *objets d'art*. In one manor house near Broadway there was a huge collection of Japanese armour. I also saw many pieces of Arita and Imari ware as well as *ukiyo-e*. In some cases, it was not easy to tell at first glance whether the objects were of Chinese or Japanese origin, but I felt nostalgic on seeing so many oriental pieces. There were also many collectors of netsuke in ivory decorated in many ways, and more discussion of netsuke than you will encounter in Japan. I was indeed frequently asked about netsuke. It was interesting that some *objets d'art*, gradually being forgotten in Japan, were so popular in England.

I think that I did pretty well in grasping my opportunities in travelling so much in England during my two years stay there. My deepest impressions were of the English countryside with its carpet of green fields, of the old towns with their historical flavour and of the simple life of ordinary British people. The chance to see the true face of Britain was a most valuable experience for me.

Travelling round Europe and meeting European royal families

As I mentioned briefly in the chapters devoted to the arts and to my studies, I also visited many countries in Europe. I shall now summarize what I did.

When my parents visited Norway I met them in Bergen as a result of the kindness of His Majesty the King. I shall never forget sailing up the fjords together with the Crown Prince and Princess of Norway (now the King and Queen) and spending a night on board ship. I was warmly entertained by their Royal Highnesses and I recall the relaxing time I had with them. Just as with the Belgian Royal family I was impressed by the strength of the friendly ties between the Japanese Imperial and the Norwegian Royal families. In Holland the Queen of the Netherlands with the Prince Consort and their children, despite their busy schedule, kindly entertained me by taking me on a cruise. While travelling in Spain I called on the King who was then staying at his villa in Majorca and lunched with Their Majesties, the King and Queen of Spain. The King, realizing that I had made the visit to the island in order to call on him, asked whether there was any place in Majorca which I particularly wanted to see after lunch. Although it was not on the original schedule I replied that I would like to see the house where Chopin lived with Georges Sand. The King asked Crown Prince Philip to arrange this and he kindly accompanied me there. I have mentioned my contacts with the families of the Grand Duke of Luxembourg and the Prince of Liechtenstein in Chapter 7 about sports.

I recognized that the warm welcome I received from European royalty was due to the friendly relations, which my parents had built up with them over the years. I realized, indeed, how fortunate I had been and the importance of continuing these ties for future generations.

I visited in all thirteen countries in Europe. It is a pity that I cannot mention them all separately. I recognized the importance of getting to know not only Britain but also European countries. I was able to see for myself that although the countries of continental Europe are part of the same land mass their history, people and cultures all differed. Britain and Japan are both separated by sea from their adjacent continents, but I could not avoid noting that the distance between Britain and the continent was short and this had led to British culture and society being greatly influenced by Europe.

CHAPTER 10

LOOKING BACK ON MY TWO YEARS' STAY

————————□————————

The English people as I saw them

In concluding this memoir I should like to say a few words about my impressions of England, and record a few of the feelings which made up my experience of Britain.

One point I should make to begin with is that in Britain the old and the new exist harmoniously side by side. Soon after my arrival, I attended the official opening of parliament and saw for myself the way in which Britain is a traditional country. At Oxford, I saw students wearing the traditional cap and gown pass in the streets youngsters in punk rock garb, but I did not feel that it was out of the ordinary. It seemed to me that both reflected the spirit of the place. This was after all a country which produced the Beatles and the miniskirt. I felt that, while the British attach importance to old traditions, they also have the ability to innovate. Take sports, for instance; there are many sports such as golf, rugby and cricket which started in Britain. The Industrial revolution took off in Britain before any other European country.

At Oxford, I could not avoid feeling the weight of tradition. I could see this in the solemn ceremonies which were performed in the same way as they had been for centuries, in the clothes which students had to wear for the entrance ceremony and the fact that the ceremony was conducted in Latin. I was impressed by the importance attached to history as shown for instance in the Latin Grace said at High Table in college and by the antique silver used there.

The college system is too complicated to explain in a few words. But I thought that the way in which students in different disciplines lived and ate together and were given the opportunity to provoke one another's intellectual curiosity was admirable. At the Gakushūin, where I studied in the humanities faculty, the different subjects were taught on different floors. Even if you were in the humanities faculty it was difficult, unless you made a major effort, to establish contacts with students studying other subjects in the same faculty. It was even more difficult to do so with students in other disciplines.

What did Oxford students think about tradition? What view did they take of the coexistence of tradition and innovation? Some students declared that their respect for tradition was no more than superficial. Some also thought it strange to be asked such a question by a Japanese, as they thought that Japan was a country where tradition was highly valued. Some older people boast that they take traditions seriously and are proud of behaving in accordance with tradition.

It was not only in my life as a student that I felt the weight of tradition. I often felt it strongly when I was invited out to British homes. In old houses I often saw portraits of the family's ancestors hanging on the walls. In some cases the walls seemed to be totally hidden by portraits and I would be told about each of those portrayed. I felt that each family wanted to preserve carefully their tangible and intangible legacies.

I am sure that I was not the only one who felt that, while at first sight there was something incompatible between the old and the new in Britain, British society had been sufficiently flexible and discerning to ensure that there was no confrontation between the two.

My second point is my belief that the British usually take a long-term view of things. I felt that the character of the British people lies in generally not forcing the pace when dealing with immediate problems and in thinking about the future implications of what they do. We can see this in the way in which buildings are put up. Let us take as an example the building of a great cathedral. Most of them took many centuries to complete. The stone mason who cut the first stones would never see the completed building, but as he loaded each stone he would see the future cathedral in his mind's eye. Cathedrals are not the only large buildings made of stone. We Japanese tend to be absorbed by what immediately confronts us. I do not think that we are very good at thinking about things in the long term. I think this can partly be explained by the difference between living in a building made of wood, which can be done relatively quickly, and one made of stone, which requires much longer to complete.

In the context of the difference between stone and wood I should mention the difference between Japan and Britain in relation to privacy. It may be due to the kind of houses they live in, but the British attach a great deal of importance to their private life and to their own space and time. In talking with British people I had the feeling that they were prepared to discuss personal matters up to a certain point, but that there were some aspects of their life on which other people should not trespass. At places such as country houses, people observe notices saying 'private', and although there is no fence or anything to stop one from going beyond people rarely go past the sign. The British like to enjoy their holidays to the full. It seemed to me that they look on their vacations as an important opportunity to store up energy for their future work. In brief, on the basis of their traditional individualist beliefs, they defend firmly what they regard as strictly personal. There is a tacit understanding that certain areas are mutually inviolable. Is not this the difference of identity between people who live in spaces which are separated from the outside by stone and those who live in spaces separated by very thin partitions made of substances like paper and wood, which can easily be penetrated by anyone?

I have already mentioned how adept the British are at social rela-tionships, and the way they show consideration for others by, for instance, holding doors open for people behind them. I was also often aware of their inconspicuous acts of warmth and sympathy towards the disabled. In this context, when in my first term I was attending a lecture by Professor Mathias in the examinations school, I noticed that the group of students who were walking and chatting in front of me moved to the side and a gap opened up. I wondered why and saw a student walking with a straight back and carrying a white stick. The group of students while continuing to walk and chat had stepped aside and allowed him to pass without any fuss. I saw this kind of thing many times. Although it seemed the most natural thing in the world, I was moved. I am sure that similar things happen in Japan, but perhaps I had not personally experienced them. It seemed to me that in Oxford disabled people could walk around the streets and live and behave with dignity. Thus, they were able to merge easily and well into the life of Oxford. It seemed to me that importance was attached everywhere in Britain to wheel-chair access and that consideration for the needs of disabled people had spread widely in Britain.

Finally, I think that I managed in my two years stay abroad to get a glimpse of the attitude of British and continental people towards 'light'. In England the winters are cold and the skies cloudy. In midwinter it was still dark at eight o'clock and it became dark again around three thirty. When I was in my rooms in college I felt the cold and the draughts coming through the cracks and often longed for the warmth of life in Japan with its well-heated rooms. One consolation in winter was the fact that the grass remained green throughout the year. If winter seemed long the spring was lovely. The daffodils, which had sprung up all over the place, formed a yellow carpet and the multicoloured crocuses poked their heads through the turf. One can readily understand why Europeans make spring itself such an important artistic theme. In Japan, perhaps because the four seasons are so distinct, the attitude towards them seems to me a little different; from *Manyōshū*[1] days the blossoms of plum and cherry have been seen as symbols of spring, and the sound of the cuckoo as a harbinger of the arrival of summer.

In Europe, sunshine contributes greatly to making people feel that the spring has arrived. With the arrival of April the hours of sunshine lengthen and there is more chance of the sun coming out. It may still be quite cold, but people enjoy sun-bathing. The many Gothic cathedrals one sees in Europe have large stained-glass windows letting in the maximum amount of light possible. I cannot

---

[1] Produced in about AD 760, the *Manyōshū* is the oldest collection of Japanese poems from the Nara period 710–784.

help but wonder if that is not a reflection of the peoples' deep yearning for light.

Light has a connection with fashion. It seemed to me that the clothes generally worn by British people were sober and lacking in colour. The fact that this did not seem out of harmony was, I thought, because it was appropriate to the British climate. The bright colours adopted by fashions in Paris and Milan seemed to reflect the brighter sunlight of the south. I went to Paris in the spring and felt that the sunlight was brighter there than in Britain. Paris buildings are beautiful not so much because they are white but because their white colour is enhanced by the sunshine.

The European approach to light and the philosophy that goes with it are rather different from that which we Japanese adopt. Light is an abstract concept and doubtless each individual has a different feeling in his heart about it. I was struck by this when back in the bright sunshine of Tokyo I began to feel my thankfulness for sunshine gradually ebbing away.

On Leaving Britain

At one of my tutorials in my last Trinity term I heard Professor Mathias say: 'Your remaining time in Oxford is fast coming to a close and will probably end like a burst of fireworks!' I took this to heart and determined to spend my last days at Oxford to the full. Fortunately, I had very largely completed my investigation of the historical materials relating to my thesis. So I wondered what there was that I still wanted to accomplish outside my research and what things I wanted to do once more. I began to think about how many more times I would be able to do the sort of things which had been part of my daily life there such as talking with my fellow students in the MCR and in hall. I began to realize that even the smallest things in my daily life had been really important to me. At the same time, I went over once again the Oxford streets which I had got to know so well; I revisited my favourite spots and took photographs of each of them. Every little street and square brought back happy memories of my two years at Oxford. If I revisited Oxford I should probably never again be able to wander round freely like a student.

The town would remain the same; what would be different would be my position in life. When I thought about things like that I was overtaken by a strange feeling of uneasiness, and wished that time would stop. Fortunately, all the places which I remember so fondly are recorded in the photographs in the albums in my study and, of course, in my head.

As my last days at Oxford became so few they could be numbered on the fingers of one hand, my friends in the MCR gave a farewell party for me in the room I had got to know so well. This took place in the evening and almost every member I knew in the MCR and those I had got to know in the JCR turned up. C, who was in charge of the MCR accounts, made a speech at the start of the party in which he recounted some 'strange' stories about my life at Oxford. He spoke about my interest in the history of transport and the fact that I had nearly all my meals in hall, which he thought 'strange'. Then he presented me with a commemorative mug in which I had to drink at least five mugs full of some liquid which he had concocted from unknown materials (I think it was a mixture of various types of liquor). I duly performed this task! I think it was pretty strong stuff! All those present asked me when I would next come to Oxford, in what way I would perform my official duties, and would I pursue my research at Oxford? Many members of the MCR took three years to complete their research papers, so there was some talk about meeting again next year if I was coming back to Oxford after the vacation. It was sad for me to have to say farewell to those whom I had got to know so well over the last two years. This had been a happy time for me – perhaps I should say the happiest time of my life – and I owed this greatly to their cooperation and consideration for me.

In this way taking so many memories away with me I left my rooms in Merton at the end of September and spent my remaining days in Britain with the Fujis at their house or in the ambassador's residence in London. I was kindly invited to farewell receptions by the Japan Society and other Anglo-Japanese organizations and I was able to express my thanks to almost all those who had helped me during my two years stay.

Looking back it seemed to me that the two years had passed in a flash but I had learnt a great deal. I had had many interesting experiences not least at Oxford. Among my experiences were, of course, doing my own laundry and ironing! I had been able to see Britain from the inside and meet many people. Through these meetings I had learnt much about British society. I had also, seeing it from the outside, reappraised my own country. All these were irreplaceable experiences for me.

On the afternoon of 10 October I left Heathrow, where I was seen off by Colonel Hall, Japanese residents in Britain and representatives of the Japanese Embassy. As the London scene gradually disappeared from view I realized that an important chapter in my life was over. A new page in my life was opening, but I felt a large void in my heart and as I stared out of the windows of the plane I felt a lump in my throat.

POSTSCRIPT

————□————

As I wrote this account of my time studying abroad and reviewed the various memories which passed through my mind, I realized that I had come to grips with all sorts of issues while I had been at Oxford. Fond memories of each scene flashed through my mind like a revolving lantern. I faced one problem in writing this book; it was seven years since I had left Oxford. Although I could remember a good deal, there were limits to the extent to which I could recall individual events. However, fortunately while I was at Oxford, I had jotted down each day what I had done and had kept these notes. I was able to put these together with the memos made by my police escort and through these I was able to recall my experiences. My diary in English, which I had written while I was staying with the Halls and which had been checked by my English teachers, was also useful and the pamphlets and leaflets about places which I had visited on my travels together with the tickets and other items, which I had kept, were a real treasure-trove. I had taken over two thousand photographs while I was at Oxford and these were very useful for reference. In addition, the official telegrams which had been sent at the time naturally provided background material. After I came home the occasional essays which I had written about my studies were also valuable memory aides and these have been incorporated into this book.

In September 1991, I revisited England to attend the Japan Festival[1] and was delighted to be able to meet once again many of those who had helped me during my time as a student. I was much gratified to receive the award of an honorary doctorate from Oxford University. I revisited Merton where I met Dr Roberts, the warden, Dr Highfield and other dons of the college and was able to get together again with some of the students whom I had known and who were pursuing their researches. I was invited to a pub by the student I mentioned earlier who had been learning to play the *shakuhachi*. As I trod the familiar streets that evening I felt that Oxford had not changed and nostalgic memories welled up within me. I want to keep these memories sacred and I look forward to the chance of returning there once again.

In conclusion, I want to reiterate my sincere gratitude both publicly and privately to all those who helped me in so many ways, eased my path and made my stay so enjoyable. In particular, I would like to express my thanks to Professor Mathias and Dr Highfield as well as Dr Morgan for their guidance and assistance with my research, to Colonel Hall who received me so kindly in his home and to others with whom I stayed while I was in Britain, to Ambassadors Hirahara and Yamazaki and the staff of the Japanese Embassy in London, and, of course, to my two police escorts.

We make many of our own memories but many are also made by others. Thanks to all the warm friendship I received while I was abroad I have lasting and happy memories of my fruitful stay in Britain.

Finally, I wish to express my thanks to Professor Naitō Yorihiro, President of the Gakushūin School, and to Professor Hayakawa Tōzō, President of the Gakushūin University, for encouraging me to recall the happy days of my youth and write these memoirs.

Prince Naruhito
Winter, 1992

---

[1] The Japan Festival in the United Kingdom in 1991 marked the centenary of the foundation of the Japan Society. The Kyoto Garden in Holland Park in London, which was opened by the Prince of Wales and the Crown Prince, is a permanent memorial of the Festival.

BIBLIOGRAPHY

———□———

Andō Nobusuke, Koike Shigeru and others, (Edited): *Igirisu no seikatsu to bunka jiten* (Dictionary of British life and culture) Kenkyusha, 1982.

Ugawa Kaoru: *Igirisu no shakai-keizaishi no tabi* (A journey through British social history), Nihon kiristokyōdan shuppankyoku, 1984.

Koike Shigeru (editor): *Igirisu,* Shinchōsha 1992.

Mikasa no Miya Tomohito: *Tomhito-san no egeresu Ryūgaku,* Bungei-shunjū 1991.

John Bergh,(translated by Kamei Akira and Tamaki Yutaka) *Daisakkyokuka no Shōgai,* Kyōdō Tsūshinsha, 1978.

In addition to guide books to Merton College and *The Story of Oxford* published by the Oxford Museum, there are other reference works such as:

Christopher Hibbert (edited): *The Encyclopaedia of Oxford,* London, 1988.

Michael Hall & Ernest Frankl: *Oxford.* Cambridge, 1981.

Anthony F. Kersting & John Ashdown: *The Buildings of Oxford,* London, 1980.

V. H. H. Green: *A History of Oxford University,* London, 1974.

Christopher Brooke & Roger Highfield: *Oxford and Cambridge,* Cambridge, 1988.

Nikolaus Pevsner: *The Buildings of England, Oxfordshire,* Middlesex, 1974.

Howard Colvin: *Unbuilt Oxford,* London, 1983.

Anton Gill: *How to be Oxbridge,* London, 1986.

Mari Pritchard & Humphrey Carpenter: A *Thames Companion,* Oxford, 1981.

John Gagg: *Canals,* London, 1982.

John Arlott: *The Oxford Companion to Sports and Games,* Oxford, 1977.

Daniel Topolski: *Boat Race,* London, 1985.

Malcolm D. Whitman: *Tennis-Origins and Mysteries,* New York, 1932.

INDEX

———□———

Personal names[1] and place names outside Oxford and London.

Abingdon, 12, 22,103
Adam, Hans, Crown Prince of
　Liechtenstein — see Liechtenstein
Akasaka Palace, 98
Akishino, Prince, 64
Albert, Prince, 83
Alexandra, Princess, 3
Alfred, King, 37, 130
Allegri Quartet, 76
Andrew, Prince, 3
Anne, Princess, 3
Ascot, 95, 96
Ashcroft, Peggy, 73
Ayer, Bruce, police escort[2], 61, 62, 76,
　145
Aylesbury, 112

Bach, J.S. 81
Bacon, Roger, police escort, (see also
　endnote 2) 61, 62, 145
Balliol, John de, 37
Balmoral, 133
Barclay, Mr (friend of Colonel Hall), 14
Bashō, Matsuo, 99

Beatles, The, 82,132
Beatrice, Queen, 13
Becker, Boris, 90
Beethoven, Ludwig van, 78—80, 82, 119
Belgians, King of the, 62, 135
Ben Nevis, 93, 94
Bergen, 135
Besselsleigh, 22
Bibury, 129
Blacker, Dr Carmen, xvii
Bodley, Sir Thomas, 105
Bonn, 82
Bonnington, Chris, 95
Borrowdale, 94
Bouchier, Dorothy, Lady (Britton), xvii
Brahms, Johannes, 18, 79, 83
Brighton, 6
Britten, Benjamin, 82
Broadway, 64
Brook, Peter, 73
Brook Shields, 68
Brooke, Professor Christopher, 101, 115
Broughton Castle, 63
Burford, 129

---

[1] The Prince's fellow students are generally referred to by an initial and as such are not listed
　in this index.
[2] There are references to 'my police escorts' on a number of other occasions, but as the
　Prince does not say which these have not been indexed.

Index

Burns, Mr, Oxfordshire County Records official, 103, 104,115
Burton, Richard, 73

Cambridge, 18, 131
Campbell, Lord, 93, 132, 133
Canterbury, 6
Carpenter, Humphrey, 104
Carroll, Lewis, 72
Charlie, Bonny Prince, 133
Charles, Prince of Wales, v, vii, 17, 75, 145
Charles I, King, 41
Chedworth, 17, 54
Cheltenham, 15
Chester, 131
Chichibu, Princess, 18
Chiselhampton, 21
Chopin, Frédéric, 136
Cirencester, 122, 129, 130
Clapham, J.H., 119
Clifton Hampden, 12
Connors, Jimmy, 90
Constable, John, 134
Corcos, Mr (Philip) and Mrs (Diana), 9, 11, 12, 20-2
Cran Montana, 96
Cranbourne, Lord, 134
Culham, 12
Curren, Kevin, 90

Defoe, Daniel, 114
Delius, Frederick, 82, 83
Diana, Princess of Wales, 17, 75
Doddington Hall, 133
Dover, 134
Dowland, John, 82
Durham, 133
Dvořák, Antonin, 80-3

Edinburgh, 17-19
Edinburgh, Duke of, see Philip, Prince
Edward, Prince, 3
Elgar, Edward, 82
Eliot, T.S., 83
Elliott, Mark

Fort William, 93
Fuji Akira, Counsellor (and Mrs), 8, 14, 19, 22-4, 53, 120, 142

Gagg, John, 11
Gakushūin, xvii, xviii, 109, 110, 145
Galsworthys, 132
Gandhi, 29, 73
George II, King, 81
Gielgud, John, 73
Glencoe, 132
Glyndebourne, 75, 120
Goring, 130
Grafton Lock, 121
Greenwich, 10
Guildhall Library, 113

Haddington, Earl and Countess of, 18—20
Hadfield, C., 124
Hall, Colonel Tom (also Halls), xvii, 3, 7, 10-17, 20-2, 54, 62, 64, 96, 108, 118, 119, 143-5
Hall, Edward, 7, 10, 15, 16
Hall, John, 7, 15
Hall, Lucy, 7
Hall, Mariette, Mrs, 7, 12, 13, 80
Handel, George Frideric, 43, 81-3
Harvey, Dr Barbara, 58
Harvey, Dr William, 41
Hastings, 6
Hawksmoor, Nicholas, 107
Hayakawa Tōzō, Professor, 145
Hayashi Tatsusaburo, 99
Haydn, Joseph, 75, 77-80, 83, 119
Headington, 117
Helsinki, 132
Henley-on-Thames, 5, 103, 130
Henrietta Maria, Queen, 41
Henry II, King, 33
Henry V, King, 90
Highfield, Dr Roger, vii, xvii, 4, 28, 29, 39, 47, 57, 63, 64, 72, 75, 92, 101, 102, 115-23, 126, 145
Hirahara Tsuyoshi, Ambassador, 1, 2, 5, 8, 55, 145

Index

Hitchcock, Alfred, 67
Holland, 13
Holst, Gustav, 84
Howard, Professor Michael, 29
Howell, Herbert, 84
Humfry, Duke, 105

Iffley, 117, 118
Iron Bridge (Shropshire), 110
Irvine, A.C., 45
Isle of Wight, 134

James I, King, 133
Japan, Emperor and Empress, (during
the Prince's stay at Oxford Crown
Prince and Princess of Japan, later
Heisei era Emperor (given name
Akihito) xiii, xvii, 62, 63, 136
Japan, Showa era Emperor (given name
Hirohito), xiii, 17, 22

Kent, Duke of, 90
Kew, 113,
Kodály, Zoltán, 43, 75
Kyoto, 99

Lake District, 20, 94
Lawrence, T.E., 72
Lean, David, 73
Lechlade, 103, 112, 123
Liddell, Dr, 72
Liechtenstein, Crown Prince of, 96, 136
Lincoln, 133
Liverpool, 132
Lloyd Webber, Andrew, 82
Loch Ness, 132
Luxembourg, Grand Duke of, 96, 136

McEnroe, John, 90
Machimura Akiko, x
Macmillan, Harold, Earl of Stockton, 35
Mahler, Gustav, 19
Majorca, 136
Mallory, George Leigh, 45, 95
Man, Isle of, 76, 77
Mansfield, Earl and Countess of, 3, 19, 20

Margaret, Princess, 3
Marlow, 6
Mary, Princess of Liechtenstein, 96
Mathias, Peter, Professor, vii, xv, xvii, 3,
5, 16, 17, 39, 47, 54, 63, 72, 87, 100-
11, 119, 126, 134, 141, 145
Maunsfield, Henry de, 44
Mendelssohn, Felix, 83
Meribel, 96,
Merton, Walter de, 41
Methuen, John, British Envoy to
Portugal 1691, later Lord Chancellor
of Ireland, 60
Mibu Motohiro, 1
Milan, 141
Miller, Sir Peter, 134
Mizoguchi Kenji, 68
Morgan, Dr, 111, 113, 145
Morris, William (Oxford motor
manufacturer) 51
Mozart, Wolfgang Amadeus, 19, 78, 80,
82, 120
Mussorgsky, Modeste Petrovich, 75

Naitō Yoshiro, Professor, 145
Nakagawa Tosu, Ambassador, 8
Needham, Professor Rodney, 16, 108
Netherlands, Queen Beatrice of the, 13,
136
Newport, 153
Northampton Norway, King of, 135
Norway, Crown Prince and Princess of,
135
Norwich, 134

O'Brien, Dr Patrick, 101
Oilly, Robert d', 118
Oman, 68
Orvieto, 131
Oswald, Sir Michael, 13
Ozu Yasujiro, 68

Paris, 141
Peterborough, 134
Pevsner, Nicholas, 117
Philip, Duke of Edinburgh, 1, 17, 18, 133

Index

Portsmouth, 134
Prague, 82, 131
Princeton, 68
Pritchard, Mary, 104
Purcell, Henry, 82

Queen Elizabeth II, 2, 3, 17, 63, 77, 95, 133

Radcot Bridge, 12
Reading, 103, 111-14
Richards, Sir Rex, 3-5, 24, 25, 28, 31, 41, 63, 72
Roberts, Dr John, 72, 145
Rossini, Giachomo, 75
Rye, 134

St John's Lock, 122
Salzburg, 82
Sand, George, 136
Sapperton Tunnel, 122
Sark, Island of, 134
Saye and Sele, Lord and Lady, 63, 131
Sayako, Princess (Nori no miya), 64
Savile, Henry, 42
Scafell Pike, 94
Schubert, Franz, 13, 76, 77, 79, 80
Scone Palace, 19
Shakespeare, William, 21, 74, 90
Shetland Islands, 122
Salisbury, 9, 10
Siena, 131
Simmonds, Dr John, 16, 17
Smith, Adam, 72
Snowdon, Mt, 94, 95
Spain, King and Queen of, 136
Spain, Crown Prince Philip of, 136
Spoht, Louis, 78, 79
Stamford, 133
Stonehenge, 9

Storry, Mrs Dorothie, 120
Storry, Dr Richard, 120
Stour, River, 134
Stratford-upon-Avon, 21, 74
Strauss, Richard, 75
Swaan, Wim, 101, 115

Tallis, Thomas, 83
Thatcher, Mrs, 3, 49, 58
Thomas à Becket, 33
Truro, 132
Tyninghame Castle, 18, 19

Ugawa Kaoru, 39, 58

Vaughan Williams, Ralph, 81-3
Victoria, Queen, 83
Vienna, 82
Visconti, 67

Wagner, Richard, 76
Wales, 133
Wallingford, 130
Walton, William, 84
Weston, Rev.Walter, 95
White Horse, The, 130
William of Durham, 37
William of Wykeham, 37
William the Conqueror, 118
Wimbledon, 15, 49, 90
Windsor, 1, 103
Wordsworth, William, 20
Wren, Sir Christopher, 31, 108

Yamazaki Toshio, Ambassador, 145
Yasuda Motohiro, Professor, 109, 110
York, 131

Zuckerman, Pinchas, 18